CAYUGA WATER DRUM WITH STICK AND MASK

The water drums and horn rattles accompany social dances. Originally wooden vessels burned out of tree knots and covered with woodchuck skin (Fenton), drums have also been made for a century or more from butter tubs and paint kegs. The pitch of the drum is controlled by the water level in the keg and the tightness of the skin. The beater is carved to fit thumb and forefinger and has a small wooden ball which sets up an echo beat. The mask is the laughing-beggar type worn by small boys when they go around the houses begging for tobacco at the Midwinter Festival (Fenton).

Drum and stick: 1624. Caledonia, Ontario, 1922. M. G. Chandler. *Mask*: The style is of the Senecas of Cattaraugus Reserve, New York, or possibly those at Tonawanda. Albert G. Heath.

The Iroquois
a Study in Cultural Evolution

BY FRANK GOULDSMITH SPECK

Cranbrook Institute of Science

BULLETIN TWENTY-THREE   SECOND EDITION

Foreword to the Second Edition

Frank Gouldsmith Speck prepared this account of Iroquois history and culture as background material for interpreting exhibits at Cranbrook Institute of Science. The first edition, issued by the Institute in 1945, found wide acceptance, and has continued in demand though now long out of print.

Dr. Speck's death in 1950, at the age of 68, ended a distinguished career in the fields of ethnology and linguistics of the fast-vanishing tribes of eastern North America. Had he lived, he might have chosen to make some minor changes in the present publication, but we cannot know this, and we re-issue it with his words unchanged.

The objects here illustrated (excepting, of course, the buildings!) are in the collections of the Institute. Two illustrations have been added in the present edition. I am responsible for the selection of all the illustrations and for their captions. In the main the selection is limited to material which is clearly from the Six Nations of the League of the Iroquois, but in some instances, as indicated in the legends, I have referred to the League certain undocumented specimens which are typologically Iroquoian. In other instances, also indicated, the specimens illustrated are surely or probably from the Huron (including the Wyandotte), an Iroquoian tribe not in the confederacy but with a similar culture. There are illustrations too of objects from the Delaware, Abenaki, and Mohican, neighboring tribes with a material culture similar to that of the Iroquois.

The greater number of Iroquoian objects in our museum were collected by Mr. Milford G. Chandler. Some, as indicated, were obtained by Dr. Speck and others. It should be observed that Mr. Chandler has not made a practice of recording data pertaining to specimens collected; such information as is presented must in most instances be considered approximate, since it was set down from his memory, sometimes more than twenty years after the (presumed) date of collection.

Mr. William P. Harris, Jr., and I made most of the photographs illustrating this paper. A few are by Mr. Gustavus Pope, Jr., and others by Mr. Harvey Croze. Editorial work is by Miss Dorothy Tyler. To all who played a part in production of the work I wish to express my appreciation for work well done.

Robert T. Hatt, *Director*
Cranbrook Institute of Science

March 30, 1955

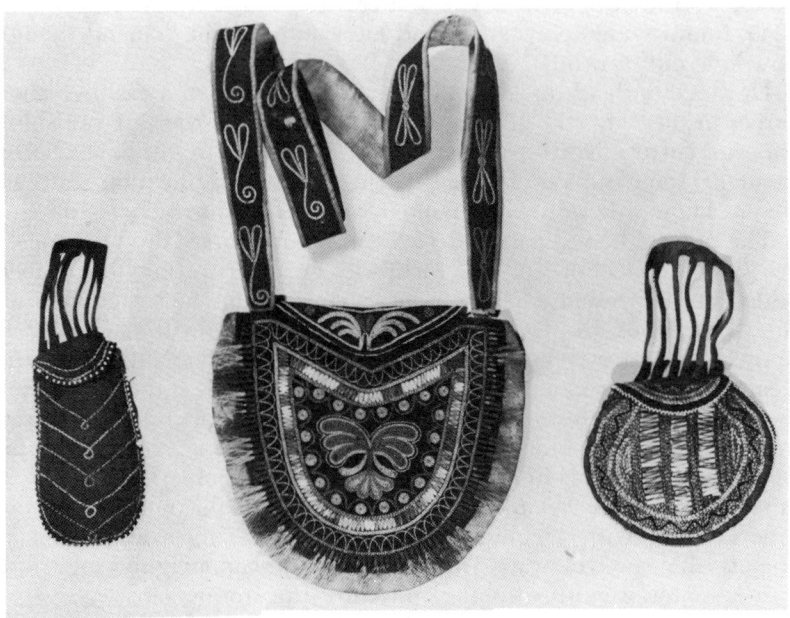

OLD POUCHES

Left: A puzzle pouch of black buckskin, moosehair decorated on one side only, and fringed with white beads. Puzzle pouches, often used for small trinkets are cleverly assembled to mask the opening. The use of black buckskin is of rare occurrence.

Center: A shoulder bag of very early type. The decoration is porcupine quill and moosehair on black buckskin, with danglers of moose (?) hair held in metal cones. The shoulder strap is lined with commercial cotton. This is probably a Huron piece though a similar piece in the United States National Museum is attributed to the Assiniboine.

Right: This puzzle purse is of buckskin, covered on both sides with porcupine quill work and edged with beads. The dyes used are at least in part commercial. Though there is a possibility of this being of Iroquois manufacture it is more typical of neighboring Algonkian tribes.

Left to right: 1794. From the Iroquois area. M. G. Chandler. Presented by Caroline Lee Pope. Depth 5 inches. 2135. Niagara Falls, N. Y., 1930. M. G. Chandler. Depth 7 inches. 982. History unknown. Presented by Joseph H. Hunter. Depth 4¼ inches.

Contents

	Page
Foreword	5
Introduction	9
The Iroquoian Linguistic Family and Population	15
Social and Civil Aspects of Iroquois Culture	26
Economic and Ecologic Aspects of Iroquois Culture	38
Iroquois Arts and Crafts	46
Iroquois Decorative Design and Symbolism	57
Ceremonial Properties of the Iroquois	65
Masks	67
Musical Instruments	77
Bowls, Spoons and Ladles	82
Wampum	84
Sacred Plants	85
Medicine Societies	86
Modern Worship of the Iroquois	87
References Cited and Consulted	89

IROQUOIS PALISADED VILLAGE MODEL

The model represents living conditions in pre-colonial times. Until sometime in the 17th century, Iroquois villages were palisaded for protection. The bark houses of the modern period were single-family units, but the longhouses of ancient times were multiple dwellings, sheltering perhaps twenty families. Villages were located on the banks of a river or near lakes or springs, for the Iroquois did not know the use of wells. Cultivated lands, divided into family plots, lay outside the stockade.

Model at Cranbrook prepared in 1931 by Everett R. Burmaster from data compiled by the Buffalo Museum of Science.

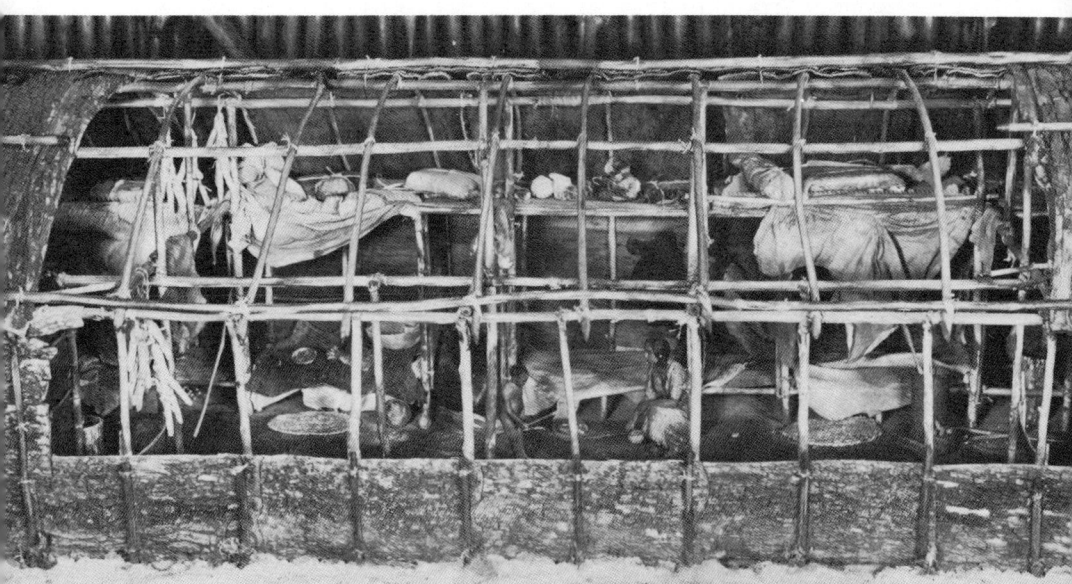

DETAIL OF ANCIENT LONGHOUSE INTERIOR

However long the longhouse there were but two doors, one at each end. Along both sides of the house were two tiers of seats, serving as bunks at night. Corn, tied in bunches, was hung from the ceiling as were also weapons, rolls of tanned deerskin, and other paraphernalia. Each apartment of the longhouse had a fire in the center and accommodated two families; one upon each side of the fire.

Model at the Cranbrook Institute of Science.

8

Introduction

When Francis Parkman in 1867 applied the phrase "Romans of the New World" to the Iroquois of the eastern Great Lakes and St. Lawrence region he produced a characterization of these Indian nations that left a lasting impression upon the minds of subsequent historians. However, it was the Jesuit missionary writers, dominated by an inflexible, intolerant attitude toward belligerent heathens, who laid the foundation for the long-lived opprobrium attaching to a people who in the mass ferociously resisted evangelization. They were the forerunners in interpreting Iroquois history and have become classic references concerning a people who possessed no means of recording their own version of the events that culminated in their defeat as powers among men.

The French pioneers and Jesuits feared and execrated the natives who resisted their conquest of land and souls. They wrote the title page of Iroquois history in red, but with one eye closed lauded the character of a large segment of the same cultural group who received their advances with open arms and hearts. That segment was the Nation of the Hurons. The Hurons go down in history in the guise of angels, the Iroquois as fiends. We do not forget, however, as history is now viewed in perspective, that the two were of one phylogeny, of one parental linguistic stock, and of one cultural horizon, and differ from each other chiefly in geographical location and the reception they gave the Fathers. The Huron collaborationists were warmly extolled by the French historians of the time, the Iroquois nationalists anathematized.

Such is our historical legacy from the seventeenth century, and the traditions of history die hard. Historians, both eyewitnesses and the secondary source writers, saw the aggressive military performances of a period and its people in magnified proportions and habitually made these the subject of record. The impressions left are almost indelible, for, as Holmes observed, we are "tattooed in our cradle with the beliefs of our tribe" when it comes to handed-down notions concerning alien peoples. Critical reëxamination of Indian culture personality in colonial times discloses that wars were horrible accidents, unavoidable in many instances by natives who were not war-minded but were persistently branded as such. An investigator who makes his approach solely by the channels of history often sees behind the narratives what was never put upon record because there were no scribes among the natives. Their side of the story has persisted only in oral tradition and tribal memory and barely reaches beyond the inner circle of tribal life.

Time, however, has changed the scene. With the advent of field investigators trained in methods of social anthropology the inner circle is opened, esoteric lore comes before the spotlight, and the audience of judges, made aware of newer values of human conduct and ideas, sits attentive. The interpretation of history takes new form, frequently radical, always original. The motives underlying the conduct of turbulent actors are considered from the angle of understanding the cultural pattern of the native group as a whole. The treatment accorded them becomes the source of subjects chosen for dissertations, which are published. The documents accumulate on the shelves of libraries and come before the eyes of scholars. The museums perform their function by exhibiting the stage settings and visual properties of the show. For those who wish to see, the epic of native culture is spread out.

Thus is begun a new era of study of America's people of the land. By such methods consideration is given to what they knew and did in the past, what happened in the period of transition after they had come into contact with Old World aliens, and what developed in the blending process that continues to the present—prehistory, protohistory, and acculturation.

The broader attitude toward the motives prevailing during the period of struggle for existence through which most small nations and "race" minorities have passed is finding a place in the thought of scholars in other fields as well. Dr. Richard H. Shryock, editor of the *Pennsylvania Magazine of History and Biography*, writes[*] for the modern historical profession: "It is too bad that all the general historians dealing with American history were not familiar with this point of view long ago." Charles Edgar Gilliam, student and writer in the field of jurisprudence, remarks[*] concerning the stumblingblock of previous historical misunderstandings: "A different attitude of mind would place a more helpful interpretation upon all recorded history—and I think each generation of men is prone to make the same mistakes over and over again because of that seemingly small but important difference of mental attitude which arises from looking at the outward and visible signs of events rather than their inward and invisible spirit. . . . Frankly, I have never seen customs of 'savage and semi-savage people analyzed from the viewpoint of human rights'."

In commenting upon the ideas expressed in this introduction Dr. William Nelson Fenton writes: "From Boas's point of view, that cultures should be described in terms of themselves, the Iroquois have never had a fair deal. Certainly there is material enough in the Deganawidah epic to argue for a society with peace, righteous-

---

[*]Correspondence, 1944.

10

ness, civil authority, and reason as its cardinal principles. Nowadays instead of Parkmanisms and Cooperisms we have economic determinism as the scholastic compulsive that motivates our students." Fenton calls attention to a pertinent passage in G. T. Hunt's *Wars of the Iroquois* (1940):

Francis Parkman's pronouncements on the Iroquois . . . are not trustworthy. Despite the brilliance of his work on New France, his fundamental misconception of the entire interracial problem, with his predilection for French sources and attitudes, invalidates his opinions concerning the Iroquois. It may at first seem strange that Parkman, who could be so impartially and keenly critical of the Jesuit institution and clerical views on worldly matters, should have adopted uncritically and quite without reservation the clerical explanation of the Iroquois. Yet it may not be strange. As depicted by Parkman, the Five Nations furnish a lurid background of fire, blood, and villainy against which to draw in bold lines the failure of New France. As has been remarked elsewhere, the Iroquois tradesman is not an especially romantic figure, and it may be that the artist in Parkman responded more readily to the Iroquois warrior. But neither the Iroquois institution nor their achievements can be thus neatly explained by innate treachery, unqualified cruelty, and insensate blood-lust. The shortcomings of a people can hardly be the reason for their greatness.*

An instance occurs in the fate of the Jesuit missionary father Isaac Jogues, who was tortured and treacherously murdered by the Iroquois in 1646, as the records of contemporary priests tell us. Jogues, earlier adopted by the Mohawk Wolf Clan, was accused by the Mohawk of spreading an epidemic among them and causing the failure of their crops, and specifically of "having concealed certain charms in a small coffer, which he had left with his host as a pledge of his return," thus causing them to be afflicted. It was determined that he should be put to death as a sorcerer. In the light of closer study it is possible to interpret their act not as a barbarous deed but as a protective expedient, undertaken in accordance with their traditional legal procedures, to rid themselves of a malignant sorcerer. If the incident is viewed thus, their formal manner of dispatching Jogues is evidence that he was not murdered but executed, in a spirit not unfamiliar to European civil and clerical courts of the time.

Other interpretations of the motives involved in the fate of Father Jogues have been offered. Hunt, in the book already cited, points out that at the time of Jogues's death in October 1646 the Mohawk were at war with the French, who had broken the peace sealed between them and the Mohawk in 1645. Jogues had previously gone to the Mohawk towns in the spring of 1646, and his welcome reflected the new peace. Shortly afterwards he departed for Montreal, leaving behind him the reliquary box of the narrative. After some months, during which the French had violated the commercial

---

*Quoted by permission of the publishers, the University of Wisconsin Press.

treaty with the Indians, Jogues returned to his mission and was killed by action of the Bear Clan. The Wolf and Turtle clans had offered to compound the case in accordance with a formality of Iroquois legal procedure, and Hunt therefore regards the Pandora box story as a subterfuge of the Mohawk to sanction their execution of the priest. Fenton, however, strikes the note of the present discussion by observing: "On cultural grounds, it may be argued that Jogues's reliquary caused his death. To Hunt, a historian, such arguments have less weight."

Notwithstanding the implications of the foregoing discussion, one must be on guard against portraying the Iroquois as a gentle folk innocent of all the drastic acts of which the *Jesuit Relations* accuse them. The tendency to exonerate bad characters may fall afoul of sentimentalism as weak as that of James Fenimore Cooper. But the modernist can acknowledge the deeds of black sheep without condemning the breed.

According to the pattern of Iroquois culture civil and religious affairs are interlocked to a degree well understood by authorities in the field. The national ego of a people may develop into a thing fearful yet defendable as noble when it is understood as explaining the convictions and teachings supporting the actions of the group.

We return to examine the priority of thought among those who have planted and nourished the idea of the Iroquois pervading general literature—that is, among those who stress the combative aspects of Iroquois culture.

C. F. Volney (1826) anticipated Parkman by at least forty years in comparing the Five Nations Iroquois with the Spartans, though he reversed the metaphor and referred to the Spartans as *les Iroquois de l'ancien monde*. Baron La Hontan ventured as early as 1703 to compare the Indians of Canada with the Greeks in respect to their songs and dances. Baron La Hontan's thus making them "have such refined notions" seemed "almost to confute his own belief of Christianity," wrote Beverly in 1722. On this basis certain ethnologists may yet be branded as infidels!

Had Parkman been a historian less typical of his age he might have stressed other aspects of Iroquois culture more than their wars. He might indeed have contemplated the already known facts concerning their social organization and ideology, hesitated to placard their nonempirical policies of control as Romanic, and christened them "Hellenes of the New World," who exhibited not a sensate but rather a socially idealistic and religiously sentimental phase of culture, as Sorokin would estimate it. Do such adjectives sound extravagant? Parkman's just renown as a distinguished interpreter of history has left an impression upon American literature not to be effaced by less renowned successors.

Cadwallader Colden, who preceded Parkman as a biographer of the league, may have been responsible for tingeing subsequent thought on Iroquois history with the high lights of war. Lewis H. Morgan, a near contemporary of Parkman, lived with the Iroquois and saw the nonmilitant side of their way of life. To be sure, the age of strife had passed, for he wrote after 1840. In his *League of the Iroquois* there is scarcely an echo of the war whoop or sinister scalp scream; rather, we hear the softer tones of chanted ritual and the prayer calls of the Long House as in a tabernacle. Horatio Hale, another product of the period, like Morgan had a gentler outlook on the life of the Iroquois and saw their society and religion rather than their wars in the foreground. In the next generation came the voluminous monographs of J. N. B. Hewitt.

These writers it seems were unconsciously preparing the way for the newborn child of history and ethnology to be called ethnohistory. Since their time this progeny of the mated sciences has grown to maturity.

The inscriptions of war are cut deeply into the literary memorials of the Iroquois League—so deeply, it would seem, that later studies of the people as living beings having common life interests may not at once soften the hard edges of those inscriptions; but nevertheless a change of attitude has occurred. Such trained explorers of culture

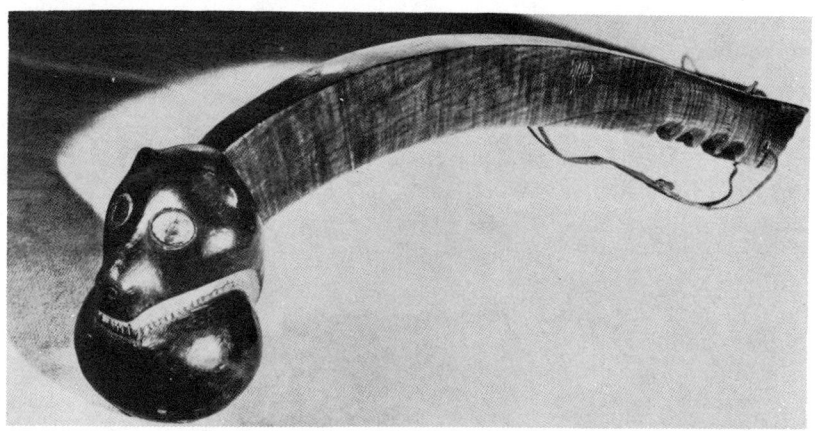

WAR CLUB

Before the trade tomahawk came into use among the Iroquois, their principal weapons were the bow, the stone tomahawk, and the war club. The war club was a heavy weapon, usually made of ironwood, with a large ball or knot at the head. It was about two feet long, the ball five to six inches in diameter. It was worn in the belt. It was used with terrible effect in close combat and was also thrown skillfully at distant objects. (Morgan).

This war club with panther head and a turtle incised on the handle was obtained from a Sioux Indian with an Iroquois wife, who said the club came from relations in New York. The club is clearly of Iroquois type and not Sioux.

3691. South Dakota, 1919. M. G. Chandler

13

as Hewitt, Parker, Goldenweiser, Barbeau, Waugh, Speck, Hunt, and Fenton, as well as such self-trained ethnologists as Beauchamp, Keppler, Converse, Boyle, and Orr have influenced modes of thought on Iroquois life by showing the inherent pacific qualities of these people. The preceptive influence of these students of Iroquois life combines science and humanity with common sense. They have seen the paramount issues involved in the formal rites, council procedures, and the philosophies, myths, chants, and epical recitations associated with virtually all political performances and social festivities. They have emphasized the bearing of the arts and crafts on the native economy of nature. And they have founded collections of Iroquois objects which are exhibited in museums and reveal the material as well as spiritual and aesthetic achievements of the Iroquois.

Thus the old, sombre picture of the Iroquois as ruthless barbarians is beginning to fade. Old customs are brought to light and the motives of men long dead are interpreted by scholars who never knew them. The panorama of Iroquois culture is unfolded as the continuous tradition of a people. For a century and a half the pertinacious Iroquois have struggled with the demons of frustration; yet despite their cultural bankruptcy they still exist as corporate bodies in Canada and New York State, preserving the consciousness of their separate identity. More numerous today than formerly, they have indeed taken the contagion of European industry and economy. But behind the changes evolving under acculturation, all too evident to most of us, there lies an inbred dynamic force abounding in self-determination.

The underlying purpose in preparing the essay that follows was to capture some of the spirit of Iroquois culture and epitomize it within the proportions of a handbook based upon and illustrated by the collections in the museum of the Cranbrook Institute of Science. Whether it is sound remains to be judged ultimately upon further and more profound evidence than a single student has been able to gather through scrutiny of the records and experience among the living people. The author hopes that the handbook may also contribute something to visual education concerning an indigenous culture conceived and matured in the fertile environment of North America.

The Iroquoian Linguistic Family and Populations

One of the long-established principles of anthropology is to classify peoples by the languages they speak. Thus tribes speaking languages which by correspondence in word stems and grammatical construction indicate that they have sprung from a common source are grouped into linguistic families or stocks. It does not follow, however, that tribes so related through common ancestry of language are necessarily identical in culture.

In eastern North America the wide territory stretching from northern Labrador, at the boundaries of the Eskimo country, southward down the coast and inland (several hundred miles in places) to North Carolina was inhabited by tribes of Algonkian* linguistic stock. The noteworthy eastern subdivisions of this group are: the Montagnais-Naskapi-Cree, in the far north; the Wabanaki of the Maritime Provinces of Canada, Maine, and northern New England; the southern New England peoples, the Delaware, Munsee, Nanticoke, and Mahican, or Mohican, of the middle Atlantic slope; and the Powhatan confederates of the Virginia and North Carolina tidewater to Pamlico Sound. These larger groups of tribes speaking related tongues comprise a score or so of politically independent tribes whose names are too well known to need repetition.

Located within the compass of the Algonkian tribal subdivisions in the region of the upper St. Lawrence and eastern Great Lakes are the tribes of Iroquoian stock. The Huron of southern Ontario were the northernmost group of the family. The Erie and Neuter occupied territory south of them in western New York State and slightly beyond. East of them in the same latitude were the nations known in history as the Iroquois proper. A region occupied by Algonkian-speaking tribes intervenes between the northern Iroquois peoples and those of the same stock encountered in Virginia south of the James River, known as Nottoway and Meherrin, and the Tuscarora, formerly of the Neuse River area. In the Appalachian highlands, south and west of the Tuscarora, is the country of the Cherokee, the southern outpost of Iroquoian speech.

In the following enumeration of the Iroquoian tribes, based largely upon Hewitt and Fenton, certain data on the past and present populations and their comparative density, as estimated by Kroeber, are incorporated.

---

*Also spelled "Algonquian," and, in the early literature, "Algonquin."

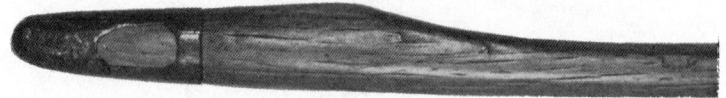

SNOWSNAKE HEAD

Snowsnakes, which among the Iroquois are commonly from five to seven feet long, are as this specimen, usually made of hickory, tipped with lead. They are hurled along an icy course, the objective being to see how far the stick may be made to go.

2157. Six Nations Reserve, 1916. M. G. Chandler. Length 60 inches.

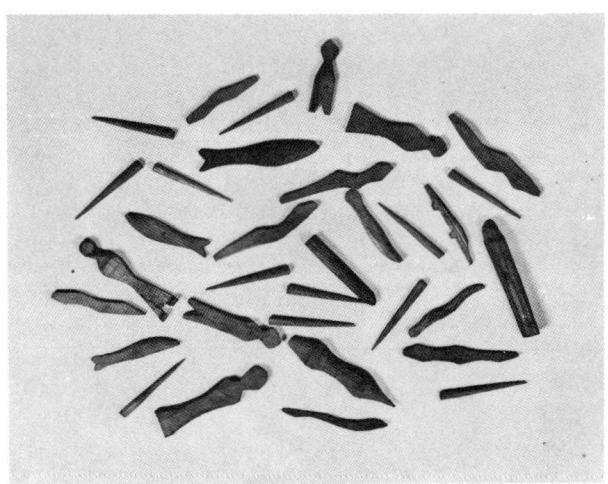

COUNTERS FOR THE BOWL GAME

The bowl game is a widespread sacred ceremonial game among the Iroquois. Two players place a wooden bowl, containing peach stones, between them, and strike it on the ground with the object of bouncing out the stones. Beauchamp (1905) figures an Onondaga counter in the form of a snake, another a geometrically carved stick. This set of thirty-six counters is from the Cayuga.

3202. Sour Springs Longhouse, Six Nations Reserve. F. G. Speck.

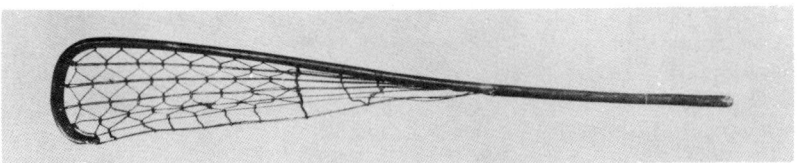

LACROSSE RACKET

Lacrosse was played with fierce competitive spirit by teams of from six to eight on a side. Each player used a single racket. This large type was used until about 1890 when it was replaced by the shorter type now in use.

1620. From Purcell Powless near Appleton, Wisconsin, 1917. M. G. Chandler. Length 53 inches.

16

ELM-BARK CANOE MODEL

The Iroquois like some of their Algonkian neighbors made temporary, hastily built canoes of elm-bark and also of spruce-bark, usually rougher in workmanship than is the case on birch canoes. These were built by the hunters for use on distant lakes and for returning home after the winter hunt. Such canoes were made up to a length of twenty-five feet. The type is now obsolete (Adney). This canoe model, one-fifth scale, is made of elm bark with gunwales, ribs and sheathing of cedar. The crossbars are of white birch, the sewing material of elm bark. It was built by Nicholas Panadis, a St. Francis Abenaki. Though the Abenaki are Algonkians the similarity of their canoes to Iroquoian ones will be found by comparing this illustration with Morgan's figure of an Iroquois canoe. (See *League of the Iroquois,* Vol. 2, plate opp. p. 3, or Fifth Ann Dept., N. Y. State Museum, plate 15.)

1918. Collected at Pierrieville, Quebec, 1927. E. T. Adney.

The Iroquoian Tribes: Areas and Populations

Laurentian (Hochelagan). This group is of the period before 1600, and inhabited the area from Montreal and Quebec to the Gaspé. Cartier is the source of information concerning the ethnology and history of this earliest known and farthest eastern Iroquoian group. His account of his expedition in 1534 gives native terms and names of villages that identify the inhabitants as Iroquois. By archaeological findings W. J. Wintemberg has proved that prehistoric groups of the same stock controlled the lower St. Lawrence and part of the gulf.

CAYUGA BOW

Bows have returned to use on the Six Nations Reserve but they are now employed for recreation.

1619. From the Atkins Family, Brantford, Ontario, 1920. M. G. Chandler.

Fenton has brought together material concerning the Laurentian Iroquoian settlements, the locations and political interrelations of the village groups, their overlordship and intertribal strife, and their final disappearance from the lower St. Lawrence before 1600, owing to reconquest of the region by the original Algonkian inhabitants.

A valuable part of Fenton's discussion is the suggestions he offers to account for Laurentian Iroquois correspondences in language with the Huron and Mohawk, the alliances and antagonisms they contracted with and against their neighbors, and correspondences in the archaeology of the St. Lawrence Iroquois sites and those of east-central New York. For the disappearance of the Laurentian Iroquois he offers four hypotheses.[*] One is that the eastern division of the group, which centered about Quebec, was aligned with the people who are found later to be the Huron—the Hochelagan band, which centered about Montreal—and gravitated southward after abandoning their villages, joined the later Iroquois, and became part or all of the Lower Iroquois. A second suggestion is that the bands around Quebec (Stadaconans) migrated to the Mohawk Valley via the "River of the Iroquois," while the Montreal bands (Hochelagans) retired inland across Ontario and ultimately joined the other Huron. A third suggestion is that "harassed by the Algonquians closest to Port Royal, and by the Iroquois to the south, both bands of Laurentians joined the Huron." Fenton's fourth suggestion is that "the Laurentians were independent peoples, neither Huron nor Lower Iroquois, that were assimilated by both of the latter." Fenton publishes a map of the Laurentian Iroquois locations of Cartier's period (1534–43).

Any further solution of the fascinating as well as classical problems of the Laurentian cultural horizon would seem by consensus to rest in the hands of archaeologists, among whom Dr. W. A. Ritchie is expected to take a leading part as expositor.

There is little of a factual nature to rely upon in any attempt to reconstruct the social and religious ways of life of the Laurentian Iroquois. One would be obliged to draw heavily upon imagination to estimate their population and its permanency, especially in the Gulf of St. Lawrence area, where they occupied fishing stations. Eskimo relationships have been hinted at and Algonkian relationships and intermixture have been assumed as inevitable in the growth of culture among the Laurentian bands dwelling between Quebec and the Gaspé.

Huron Confederacy. This confederacy, which before 1650 inhabited southern Ontario southeast of Georgian Bay to Lake Simcoe,

[*]See Fenton (1940A, pp. 175–77).

comprised four related nations—the Bear, Deer, Cord, and Rock nations—which had political individuality. Fenton gives them a total population of 30,000 in 1636, whereas Kroeber follows Mooney in allowing them 18,000, though he thinks the figure too low. Kroeber estimates their territory to have covered 1392 square kilometers, with a population density of 12.90 per hundred square kilometers. His estimates include the Tionontati, the Tobacco Nation.

By 1650 the Huron confederates were broken up by the Iroquois and dispersed. Remnants of the depopulated villages were made captive and adopted by the Iroquois and lost their original identity. Between 350 and 400 survivors live at Indian Lorette, near Quebec.

Tobacco Nation (Tionontati). The Tobacco Nation before 1650 inhabited southern Ontario, south and west of the Huron Confederacy. Population estimates and density are included with those of the Huron by Kroeber. They shared the fate of the Huron at the hands of the Iroquois. There are several small bands of descendants bearing the proper name of Wyandot (Wendat or Huron), one in Anderdon Township, Essex County, Ontario, and another, numbering about 250, combined with the Seneca in the Quapaw Agency in northeastern Oklahoma.

Neutral Confederacy (Attiwandaronk). This confederacy comprised at least three tribes, occupying the Niagara peninsula from Detroit to the Genesee River. Estimates give them from 10,000 to 12,000 population in some forty villages, with a population density of 16.80 per hundred square kilometers. By 1652 they also were dispersed or incorporated into the Iroquois.

Erie (Cat Nation). The Erie inhabited, before 1650, the shore of Lake Erie from southwestern New York to the present site of Cleveland. Mooney and Kroeber list the population as 4000, with a density as low as 3.99 per hundred square kilometers. Fenton raises the total to 8000 or 10,000.

Fenton (1940A) states: "We know very little about them because no Caucasian reached their country until after their dispersion." He discusses one of the deep-rooted sources of dissension among historians concerning the identity of the Black Minquas, who came down to trade with the Dutch and the Swedes on the Delaware as early as 1643.

Wenro. The Wenro inhabited southwestern New York, east of the Erie people, before 1640. Fenton reviews their history as an eastern member of the Neutral Confederacy, their abandonment of domain to the Seneca, and their migration to the Huron.

19

Susquehanna (Andaste, Conestoga). Before 1675 this tribe occupied the Susquehanna watershed of central Pennsylvania. Fenton makes two groups of the Susquehanna: the Andaste (Susquehanna proper) on the lower river at the falls and the "big flats people" on the north branch above Wyoming. The former he identifies with the White Minquas of the Dutch and Swedes on the Delaware and the Conestoga of the later English. His exposition of the facts recorded in the history of Pennsylvania and Maryland makes clear records that have been a source of confusion to many ethnologists and most historians. Kroeber, after Mooney, estimates the number of the Susquehanna at 5000, with a population density of 7.12 per hundred square kilometers.

Fenton interprets history as revealing a movement of the northern Iroquois from the Appalachian plateau of New York, following the watercourses, to the piedmont above Chesapeake Bay, observing that: "On the lower Susquehanna, as on the St. Lawrence, Iroquoians were expanding at the expense of Algonquians when Europeans arrived."

In 1675 the Susquehanna Iroquoians were defeated and dispersed by combined attacks of Marylanders and Virginians with Iroquois.

Iroquois Confederacy. The Iroquois Confederacy, or League of the Five Nations (Six Nations after 1722), inhabited New York State from the Hudson to the St. Lawrence and to Lake Erie. The population was 5500 at the time of discovery (1600), according to estimates of Mooney and Kroeber, with a population density of 7.49 per hundred kilometers.

The population of the original tribes now residing in New York State, Ontario, and Quebec, summarized from Fenton's 1940 figures, totals 17,000. The tribal enumerations are given below.

	1940
MOHAWK	
(Inhabiting from the Mohawk Valley to Montreal)	POPULATION
Oka, or Lake of Two Mountains Band, west of Montreal . . .	400
Caughnawaga Band, at La Chine Rapids near Montreal . . .	2200
St. Regis Band, New York and Province of Quebec, on both sides of St. Lawrence River	1550
Deseronto Band, Bay of Quinte, Ontario	1400
Gibson (Watha) Band, migrants from Oka, near Bala, Georgian Bay, Ontario	150
Six Nations Reserve, near Brantford, Ontario	1900
Total	7600*

*The existence of a small migrant group of Iroquois (Mohawk) in Alberta has been generally overlooked by enumerators of the population. A. F. Chamberlain (1904) quotes historical information showing that in 1804 some Iroquois *voyageurs* had penetrated to Athabasca River and settled, leaving 82 descendants there in 1897 on Michel's Reserve near Edmonton, with 66 descendants living in 1903. The Canadian census gives 147 in 1924, known as Paul's Band.

	1940
ONEIDA	POPULATION
(Inhabiting east-central New York)	
Nonreservation band near Oneida	90
Oneidatown, near London, Ontario	780
Green Bay, Wisconsin	2000
With Onondaga near Syracuse	150
Six Nations Reserve, near Brantford, Ontario	386
Total	3406

	1940
ONONDAGA	POPULATION
(Inhabiting central New York)	
Onondaga Band, near Syracuse	500
Six Nations Reserve, near Brantford, Ontario	375
Total	875

	1940
CAYUGA	POPULATION
(Inhabiting Finger Lakes, central New York)	
Six Nations Reserve, near Brantford, Ontario	1000
Cattaraugus reservation, southwest of Buffalo	200
Total	1200

	POPULATION
SENECA	1940
(Inhabiting western New York from	
Seneca Lake to Lake Erie)	
Six Nations Reserve, near Brantford, Ontario	200
Tonawanda Band, east of Buffalo	600
Cattaraugus Band, Cattaraugus Creek, southwest of Buffalo . .	1500
Allegheny Band, Allegheny River, Salamanca, New York . . .	900
Cornplanter Band, Allegheny River below Pennsylvania line . .	30
Total	3230

The TUSCARORA after 1722, when they were received by the Oneida as the sixth nation of the League, had a population of 800 in New York and Ontario. (See below.)

Nottoway. This tribe is mentioned in early accounts as inhabiting southeastern Virginia, near the Nottoway River. Mooney and Kroeber give 2200 as the population of Nottoway and Meherrin, with a density of 22.90 per hundred square kilometers. Mooney writes that they were linguistically closely cognate to the Tuscarora. Several score of this tribe lingered on in the region under a female leader, or "queen," as late as 1825.

Meherrin. Mooney estimated the Meherrin, living along the Meherrin River on the Virginia–North Carolina border, to number in 1669 approximately 180 souls. Kroeber's estimate includes the Nottoway. (See above.) Fenton identifies the Meherrin with the Susquehanna who fled south to escape the Iroquois, accepting Bushnell's version of official colonial documents tracing them to the

Conestoga expulsion of 1675. Mooney, however, considers that only a part of this band was composed of the expelled Susquehanna. It was the fate of the Meherrin in part to be exterminated in Bacon's Rebellion, in part sold as slaves (Hunt, 1940).

Tuscarora. The Tuscarora, inhabiting the Neuse River country in North Carolina before 1711, numbered 5000 according to Mooney and Kroeber, with a population density of 52.60 per hundred square kilometers. After their defeat and expulsion from North Carolina in 1712 the Tuscarora migrated to the Iroquois country and settled among the Oneida. They were adopted into the League of the Five Nations about 1753.

According to the 1940 enumeration there are now about 400 Tuscarora near Niagara Falls, New York, and about 400 with the Six Nations Iroquois in Brant County, Ontario.

Cherokee. The Cherokee of the southern Appalachian summit, eastern Tennessee, southwestern Virginia, western North Carolina, and northern Georgia are estimated by Mooney and Kroeber to have numbered 22,000 in the period of early contact with Europeans, with a population density of 16.30 per hundred square kilometers.

The Cherokee have proved to be a somewhat difficult group to allot to a position in prehistory as well as in culture in relation to the other Iroquoian-speaking divisions. Kroeber (1939) does not give them a place in the southeastern culture area, for reasons that seem valid. They do not show close cultural relations with the kindred Iroquois of the north or with the Tuscarora east of them. Occupying a true mountain habitat in an ecological setting more typical of central New York, the Cherokee seem to have developed a somewhat independent phase of mixed composition derived from the southeast, the Ohio region, and their probable Siouan predecessors in the highlands.

While it may be expected that analogies of some general character exist between the Cherokee and the northern Iroquoians, no progress has been made in the attempt to resolve the two cultural phases to a common foundation. The link of language is the binder by which relationship is traced. The routes of migration followed in the course of Iroquoian dispersion still defy explanation. Archaeology holds the answer.

As Kroeber points out, Cherokee culture had indirectly absorbed a relatively large series of Caucasian elements before their territory had been seriously invaded. This factor adds considerably to the difficulty of analyzing their culture. Finally, in 1838, the Cherokee Nation was forcibly removed by federal order from the home territory in the Appalachians to Indian Territory, now Oklahoma, where they constitute one of the Five Civilized Tribes. At present there are about 2000 Cherokee in western North Carolina and approximately 30,000 in Oklahoma.

A number of interesting facts can be gleaned from a study of these population totals for the Huron-Iroquois groups between the periods 1600 to 1650 and from 1650 onward. One is that the prehistoric period of intertribal strife that provided the incentive for the peace plan put into effect by Deganawidah, as traditional history relates, disturbed the population balance of the widely diffused Iroquoian settlements. Another is that the confederacy pattern, so strong in Iroquoian culture, produced a series of alliances of tribes and settlements in the different inhabited sectors, and that these alliances in turn absorbed and gave forth populations. And finally we see how the wholesale adoption of survivors of one confederation into another supplies the gross residuum for the succeeding phase of the sequence in the rise and fall of alliances. As the last phase of the sequence the historic League of the Iroquois or Six Nations would seem to owe its population maximum to the adoption policy that was one of its very foundation principles.

It is generally thought by ethnohistorians that the northern Iroquoian peoples were detached migrants pushing northward into Algonkian territory and that they followed the Appalachian highlands until they reached the eastern Great Lakes area and thence expanded to form the divisions noted. In the migrations, or perhaps better the drifts, toward the east and north, some divisions separately settled in the southern highlands and beyond, becoming the historic Cherokee, Tuscarora, and Virginia Iroquois-speaking fragments. However, one can proceed only so far in making reasonable surmises from comparative ethnographical and linguistic evidence.[*] As for an earlier area of common habitat for the Iroquoian family, Wissler voices the notion of some anthropologists that the Iroquoians and Caddoans (Pawnee) once dwelt in the Lower Mississippi Valley precincts as cultural neighbors. The two linguistic families possess some common peculiarities of grammatical structure.

Ghostly shadows of common Iroquois and Pawnee properties in essential religious beliefs and practices hover in the background, while the bones of skeletons rattle in the foreground of excavations proceeding until recently, to keep ethnologists and archaeologists awake to problems of prehistoric culture emergence from the midvale of the Mississippi. A conjuror in the science of culture history

---

[*]Quite alone among anthropologists, D. G. Brinton (*The American Race,* 1891) located the "primitive" home of the Iroquoian stock in the region between the lower St. Lawrence and Hudson Bay. One need not linger to discuss this notion now.

UPPER CAYUGA LONGHOUSE AT SOUR SPRINGS

From the band associated with this longhouse on the Six Nations Reserve came many of the specimens figured in this booklet. The longhouse dates to 1877.

INTERIOR OF THE SOUR SPRINGS LONGHOUSE

The benches along the walls are for spectators. Men with turtle rattles sit astride the benches, beating the edge of the shell against the bench top. Note how this has produced polished areas on the bench to the left of the stove.

Photographed October, 1943.

may yet produce a valid explanation if his magic is not exhausted before the archaeologists come forth with concrete testimony to settle the theory of relationship. Weer (1937), with the acumen of an ethnohistorian, epitomizes and interprets Iroquoian history along similar lines.[*]

Historical tradition is silent except for one legend recorded by Wissler, who was told by a Pawnee Indian, now long dead, that in the remote past the Iroquois and the Pawnee were neighbors and friends. Wissler cites also a tradition of conflict over boundaries of influence arising between the Iroquois and Pawnee and settled by a decision that in future the Pawnee should remain west of the Mississippi and the Iroquois east of it. When student activity in pure research can be turned wholeheartedly in this direction a solution may be forthcoming—one that will harmonize the data of philology, archaeology, and ethno-ecology.

---

[*]The most recent words on Iroquois migration are by J. B. Griffin and B. S. Kraus. Kraus (1944) notes the grounds upon which a homogeneous development of so-called "Iroquoian cultural characteristics from a general Woodland pattern is assumed." He does not consider "the traditional theory of an Iroquoian migration up the Ohio River into their historic northeastern position" to fit the facts. He cites Griffin, in an article read before the New York State Archaeological Society in 1941, as holding a similar view, and disposing of the hypothetical migration from the southwest. Without allowing for linguistic evidence, Kraus tentatively defines the Iroquois as "an early Woodland people in the northeast who were subjected to certain widespread cultural waves such as Hopewellian and Mississippian" and other cultural contacts, in response to stimuli from which they gradually attained the stage of development designated by the term "Iroquoian Aspect." Griffin (1943) has summarized his views on the migration question in a recent and profound treatment. After reviewing Parker's conclusions in respect to the northern migration of the Iroquois, he undermines the force of the argument of linguistic relationship between Caddoan and Iroquoian languages as an "excellent working hypothesis" only, as Sapir, who discovered the resemblance of the two, implied. Griffin attempts to show that "present evidence offers little archaeological support for the hypothesis of an Iroquoian migration from the mouth of the Ohio area into the northeast." The Fort Ancient and Iroquois cultures show fundamental similarities; Iroquoian culture probably has "an underlying basic connection with northeastern Woodland occupation and was strongly influenced by a diffusion of cultural traits from the southeast." This statement stands as a starting point for further exploration into cultural backgrounds of the Appalachian area.

Social and Civil Aspects of Iroquois Culture

For over a century the principles involved in Iroquois social organization and civil government, and especially in the perfection of the historic confederacy known as the League of the Iroquois, have challenged the pens of essayists writing in both Europe and America. They have made able attempts, based upon facts and fancies drawn from sources in the *Jesuit Relations* down through nineteenth-century historical writers, directed toward dissection of the extraordinary system of political control that grew up in Iroquoia, as the home territory of the Iroquois has been called. The group self-government of the Iroquois has impressed most of these writers as embodying surprisingly modern conceptions of democratic rule.

The relatively wide representative election, senatorial plurality, and absence of hereditary sovereigns in the Iroquois government have led ethnologists indulging in analysis of their civil life to compare it with that of tribes of the northwest coast, the southeast, the southwest, Mexico, Peru, and even that of peoples of the Old World. In these comparisons the Iroquois have invariably been accorded a high standing as organizers and statesmen. "The League of the Iroquois," writes Jenness of the National Museum of Canada, "would have extended its sway from the Great Lakes to the Atlantic by the subjugation of the Algonkians had not the expansion of European colonists checked its progress. Even though it never reached full blossom it will always remain a monument to the political genius of the Iroquois people."

Some of the known facts upon which such generalizations are based may be cited.

First of all, the Iroquois were, and still are, a decidedly democratic people. Chiefs earned their recognition to experience in dealing with issues of public concern and to such qualities as valor, dignity of bearing, eloquence, moral uprightness, sincerity of purpose in public service, incorruptibility, and a pleasing personality. A chief was required to have an extensive knowledge of the teachings of the ancient faith and ability to lead religious as well as civil ceremonies. The office was held for life, pending good behavior and devotion to duty, but was not hereditary.

The chiefs, elected from certain families within each clan comprising the tribe, numbered forty-nine or fifty. During their installation in office a long ritual was intoned for the council in session by chosen speakers—an impressive metrical recitation requiring some hours, and known as the Roll Call of the Chiefs.

26

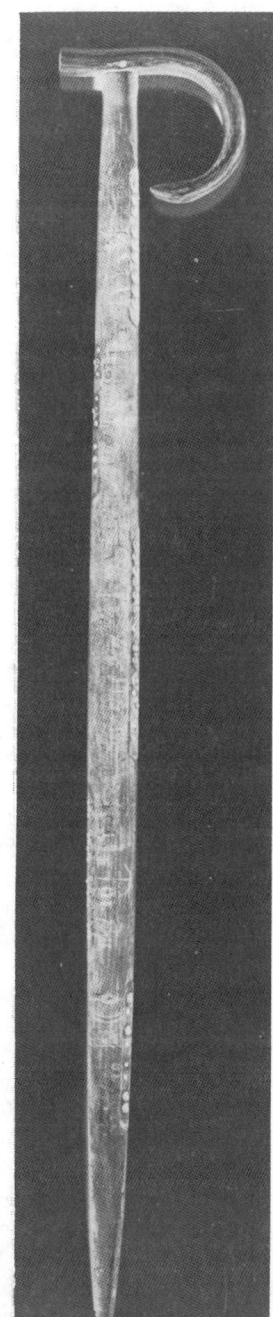

CONDOLENCE CANE

This unique cane records pictographically the hereditary chiefs of the League of the Five Nations and was used by the Lower Cayuga band on the Grand River as an aid to memory in the long recital of the Condolence Ceremony, at which new chiefs are installed. Apparently made about 1860, it was obtained from its last holder, Andrew Spragg, the Cayuga ritual singer. Several replicas of this cane have recently been made on the Six Nations Reserve and elsewhere.

For a full report on this specimen, see: *The Roll Call of the Iroquois Chiefs*, by William N. Fenton, Cranbrook Inst. Science Bull. No. 30, 1950. (Also issued as Smithsonian Misc. Coll., Vol. 111, No. 15.)

1914. Six Nations Reserve, about 1919. M. G. Chandler.

In the epic of Deganawidah, architect of the league, the names of the original founders of the confederacy are given with their meanings in the order in which they, as chiefs of the five Iroquois tribes, accepted the inspired plan for peace in union conceived by Deganawidah. They formed the original council of chiefs, never changed with respect to their number. The founders' names have been retained as something akin to titles for the positions their owners held in the first council of the league. When one of the original forty-nine or fifty offices became vacant it was filled by a properly qualified successor who took the name-title of his predecessor.

This system, founded over four centuries ago, has not changed in content or function. The chiefs, better known in literature as sachems, carry on the title names, prestige, and duties of the founders of their offices, and their qualifications must conform to the limitations of family, clan, and tribal descent possessed by the founders. Thus the pattern of the first league council is an unbreakable tradition of ancestry imposed upon political posterity.

It should be noted that the languages spoken by the five nations organizing the league—Mohawk, Onondaga, Oneida, Cayuga, and Seneca—are all employed without restraint of custom in the deliberations of the chiefs. Nevertheless, the Mohawk tongue has acquired in official use an ascendancy traceable to the political priority of the Mohawk tribe in the conception and organization of the confederacy; and priority and seniority are strong sentiments in the breasts of the Iroquois.

Mention has been made of families, clans, and phratries within the tribes. These unit groups in the Iroquois social system may be briefly defined. The family comprises individuals related by blood. The clan is a grouping of families tracing descent through the maternal line. The Iroquois did not marry within the same clan. The clan was divided into maternal families, each of which comprised a headwoman, known as the matron, and her immediate male and female descendants and their issue continuing in the female line. The average maternal family numbered from fifty to two hundred persons, grouped into individual families of husband, wife, and children. The phratry, more technically known as the moiety, or half, was a grouping of clans into two divisions related to each other in certain ways. Together the two divisions constituted the tribe.

Slightly variant forms of this general pattern characterized all the Iroquoian tribes of which we have sufficient knowledge to speak. In the formation of the League of the Iroquois this pattern was extended to cover the allied tribes, usually referred to as nations, implying that they were related to one another as clans and phra-

28

tries (moieties) were to each other. The clans, and some of the moieties, of the confederated tribes usually had names derived from animals, which served as their emblems.

The clans are thought by some ethnohistorians to have constituted in some remote period separate villages, which later became aggregated through intermarriage into mixed villages. Scholarly dissertations have been written about the clans and their relation to the moieties.

A tentative list of clan and phratry (moiety) subdivisions of the northern Iroquoian nations may be drawn up from the records of Morgan, Hewitt, Barbeau, Goldenweiser, and Speck, the last named for the Cayuga, Canadian Mohawk, Oneida, Seneca, and Onondaga only. Changes brought about by time, separation, decline of native institutions, absorption, extinction of families, intermarriage among nations, and adoption of alien tribes having clan affiliations of their own account for discrepancies in some of the series.

CLAN AND PHRATRY SUBDIVISIONS OF NORTHERN IROQUOIAN NATIONS

MOHAWK (three clans). Moiety 1, turtle; moiety 2, bear, wolf (Six Nations Mohawk).

ONEIDA (three clans). Moiety 1, wolf; moiety 2, turtle, bear (Oneidatown, Ontario).

ONONDAGA (nine clans). Wolf, tortoise, bear, deer, eel, beaver, ball, plover (snipe·), pigeon-hawk. (From Hewitt.) Wolf moiety 1, big wolf, small wolf, turtle, snipe, eagle, eel; two clans moiety 2, deer, bear, hawk. (From Speck, notes on Canadian Onondaga.)

SENECA (nine clans). Wolf, bear, beaver, turtle, hawk, sandpiper (snipe), plover (killdeer), deer, heron. (From Hewitt.) Wolf moiety 1, turtle, wolf, unidentified clan, bear; moiety 2 (no animal name), sandsnipe, deer, fast-flying hawk, eel. (From Speck, notes on Canadian Seneca.)

CAYUGA (ten clans). Wolf moiety 1, heron, wolf, plover, snipe; turtle moiety 2, deer, ball, snapping turtle, big bear, suckling bear, younger bear.

HURON, or WYANDOT (nine clans, Oklahoma). Moiety 1 (deer phratry), deer, bear, porcupine, beaver; moiety 2 (turtle phratry), big turtle (snapping turtle?), prairie turtle (box turtle?), small striped turtle (painted turtle?), hawk; odd clan, not in either moiety, wolf. (From Barbeau, 1915.)

HURON (Indian Lorette, Province of Quebec, Canada). Turtle, bear, deer, wolf. (From Barbeau, 1917.)

Powell (1880) adds sea snake to the list and names four turtle clans; Hewitt, quoting Connolley (1899), gives five turtle subdivisions.

NEUTRAL, ERIE, and TOBACCO. No records.

Morgan, Hewitt, Mooney, Bloom, and Gilbert should be referred to for clan lists of the southern Iroquoian nations. A brief list is given here.

CLAN AND PHRATRY SUBDIVISIONS OF SOUTHERN IROQUOIAN NATIONS

TUSCARORA (seven or eight clans). Bear, wolf (gray and yellow), turtle, beaver, deer, eel, snipe. (From Hewitt.)

CHEROKEE (seven clans, anciently fourteen). Wolf, deer, bird, paint, *sahani*, *gatagewi*, *gilahi*. (From Mooney, 1906.)

NOTTOWAY and MEHERRIN. No records.

LARGE LOGS OF THE SOUR SPRINGS LONGHOUSE
Some of the pine logs are sixteen inches in diameter. The bottom tier is of oak.
Photographed October, 1943.

Any attempt to summarize the structure of Iroquois society and the league must have serious shortcomings, for the sources are numerous and not all agree in the data recorded or the interpretations of such data. An extract from Jenness's *The Indians of Canada* (1934) has been chosen as giving a concise and reasonably accurate summary.

The council that administered affairs of the league was composed of nearly fifty chiefs or sachems, all of equal rank, and all selected from the maternal families. They assembled at irregular intervals, whenever necessity arose, to arbitrate on intertribal problems, to receive embassies, and to decide on peace or war with outside tribes. Being federal officials, they possessed no legal authority in matters that concerned only a single tribe or clan. . . . The method of selecting a sachem was peculiar. His title was hereditary in some maternal family, so that the choice of a representative was limited. The matron of that family selected a candidate after consultation with other women of her family and clan; her selection was ratified, first by the sachems of the same phratry, then by the sachems of the opposite phratry, and finally by the entire council of the league, which called a great intertribal festival to install him in office. The same matron had power to depose him again if he failed to uphold the dignity of his position. . . .

The authority possessed by the matrons . . . would seem to constitute them the ultimate "powers behind the throne" in the political life of the Iroquois. It has even induced some writers to call their system of government a true matriarchate, i.e., a state that was ruled by women. . . . If women among the Iroquois enjoyed more privileges and possessed greater freedom than women of other tribes, this was due, not so much to their matrilinear organization . . . as to the important place that agriculture held in their economic life, and the distribution of labour. . . . The League of the Iroquois seems really to have been a male oligarchy in which each member of the governing council of fifty had to submit to more or less supervision by the women of his maternal family, principally to the supervision of one woman, its head.

Quite apart from this supervision by the women, however, the council suffered from another and more serious limitation. Its members obtained their position by birthright, not by military prowess or ability in other ways; and while they might declare peace or war in the name of the whole league, they could not control ambitious individuals who sought profit, revenge, or renown through sudden attacks on neighbouring peoples. Many of the so-called wars of the Iroquois seem to have been irresponsible affairs, organized and conducted without the consent and often without the knowledge of the council; for since the sachems were civil chieftains, not necessarily leaders in warfare or gifted with military talents, it was easy for a warrior who had gained a reputation for skill or valour to muster a band of hunters and start out on the warpath without notice. . . . There arose in consequence a group of warrior chiefs who attained considerable influence and sometimes rivalled the sachems themselves. It was the warrior chiefs, indeed, not the sachems, who won most fame and honour during the Revolutionary War.

Even if the council had not been subject to these limitations, it was clearly impossible for so large a governing unit . . . to weld the various tribes and clans into a co-ordinated body politic. Only too often the tribes acted independently, so that one could be at peace with Algonkian neighbours who were being vigorously harassed by the others. As long as the league had only feeble Indian tribes to contend against it flourished and extended its boundaries, replacing losses in warfare by the wholesale adoption of captives; but when it

31

encountered European forces accustomed to military discipline and unified under a single command, the looseness of its organization brought about disjointed action and hastened its disruption and downfall.

Law and order within the Iroquoian confederacies lay wholly within the jurisdiction of the tribes, resting in the final analysis with the individual villages. The penalty for treason or witchcraft was death, after summary trial and conviction before a council of the villages; but compounding was permissible and usual in the case of all other offenses. "They have only one method of justice for injuries, which is that the whole village must make amends by presents. For a Huron killed by a Huron, they are generally content with thirty presents; for a woman forty are demanded, because, they say, women can not so easily defend themselves . . . for a stranger, still more are exacted;

THE OLD COOKHOUSE AT SOUR SPRINGS

This cookhouse is of the old type, with a hole in the roof instead of a chimney. On the other side of the longhouse the Upper Cayuga have built a more modern structure for preparation of the feasts.

Photographed October, 1943.

because they say that otherwise murders would be too frequent, trade would be prevented, and wars would too easily arise between different nations." (*Jesuit Relations.*). . . . Minor offenses were punishable in the same way as murder, but for refractory individuals who continually disturbed the tranquility of the community there loomed in the background outlawry, which deprived them of all legal protection and permitted anyone to kill them on sight. On the whole, public opinion and the knowledge that the entire village would be held responsible for wrong-doing seem to have proved adequate safeguards, and the domestic life of the Iroquoians was probably no less peaceful than our own. Theft was comparatively rare, for land was the property of the community, surplus food was commonly shared with needier neighbours, the long bark dwelling belonged to the maternal family, and personal property like the tools and weapons of the men, the household goods and utensils of the women, were so easily replaced that they possessed little value. Practically the only objects open to theft were the strings of wampum beads that served both as ornaments and currency; but such was the community of spirit of the Iroquoians, so little did they esteem individual wealth, that a multitude of beads brought neither honour nor profit except so far as it gave the owner an opportunity to display his liberality by lavish contributions to the public coffers. (Pages 135–39.)*

Elsewhere in his book Jenness writes: "The Iroquois, with a keen sense of democracy, permitted no social grading in their communities, no inequalities of rank, no inheritance of superior status. With an equally keen political sense, they subordinated their villages, clans, and phratries to the compact tribal units, and then federated the tribes into nations." With vivid imagery he likens their *régime* to "the glow of sunrise in an Arctic winter faded away before it reached full brightness."

There is no lack of reference, past and present, to the freedom the Iroquois exercised in adopting captives to replace loss of population. Free admission to their families and tribes was accorded to supplicants seeking the benefits of union with them. Whole tribes found a haven of refuge within the pale of the confederacy during its era of expansion from the early eighteenth century onward. Thus the Tuscarora were incorporated in 1722 and the Delawares, Tutelo, and Nanticoke between 1762 and 1765. Captives taken in combat were often sacrificed as a war measure, but it was also customary to adopt them into families, with full standing as members of clan and tribe, and to give them native spouses. The open-door policy of the Long House did not exclude Europeans, and Kroeber (1939) thinks the league became most successful in historic times largely because of Caucasian relations; that it would not have been so populous, cohesive, or permanent under purely native conditions.

Kroeber finds that by comparison with others the Iroquoian confederacies took form upon purely native bases and that they lagged little if any behind the degree of development of the southeastern confederacies. The spirit of Iroquoian culture at large shows a clear tendency to organize peoples into confederacies. In the period of first contact a Huron confederacy comprising four tribes existed around Lake Simcoe, Ontario, and another arose among the Neutrals around Lake Erie, but both succumbed to the inroads of the League of the Iroquois before the close of the seventeenth century. The Erie, then dwelling adjacent to the Neutrals, who remained outside the confederacies, shared the fate of the Huron and the Neutrals, as did the nonallied Tobacco Nation and the Conestoga.

---

*Quoted with the permission of the National Museum of Canada.

CRADLEBOARD

The back is carved and painted in a style typical of Canadian Mohawks living at Desoronto and the St. Regis Iroquois of northern New York State. The clan is identified by the beavers at the bottom. The cleat at the upper end is carved to resemble a modern chair round, which was frequently used on this type of cradleboard. There is a small shelf on the front that served to support the child's feet.

9107. Desoronto, Canada. J. Kirk Whaley. Height 30¼ inches, width 14¼ inches.

34

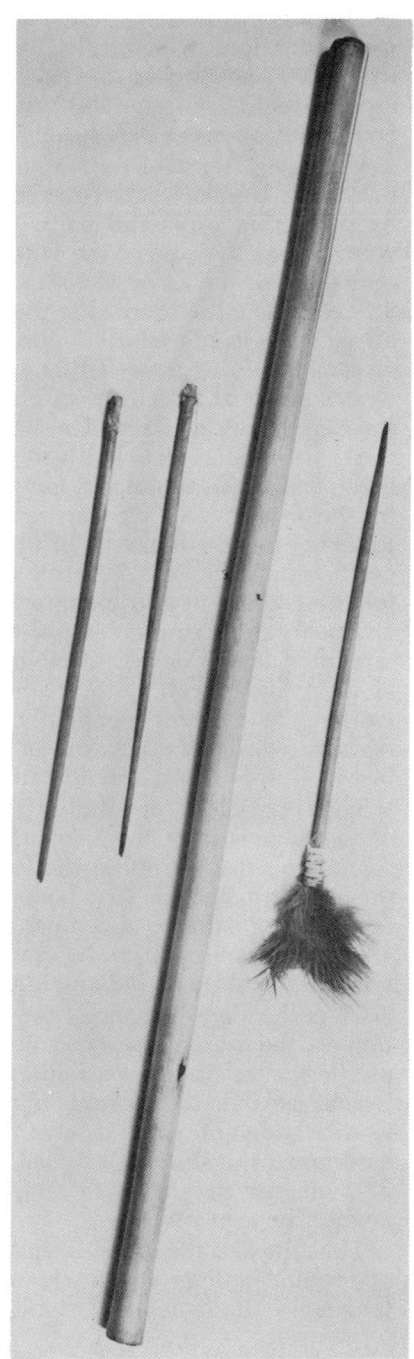

BLOW GUN AND DARTS

The Cayuga blow gun of a hollowed swamp alder stem, was used to shoot robins out of cherry trees when the fruit was ripe. Though not now used by the Iroquois they were so employed until about 1875. Morgan writes of blow guns six feet long. This one is but 27 inches.

3198. Six Nations Reserve. F. G. Speck.

The league, or Long House in the speech of the Five Nations, is something upon which to let the imagination dwell. Let us attempt a skeletal plotting of the idealistic ground plan upon which it reposed as the supreme institution in control throughout New York State until after the American Revolution.

The Long House of the league stood as a magnified working symbol of the Iroquois bark-covered long house habitation, surrounded by protecting walls and palisades, its two doors opening east and west, one at the side of the Hudson, the other near Lake Erie. The north side of the Long House, as a topographical symbol, faced the St. Lawrence, the south side the Susquehanna. This areal structure, housing the five families of united nations, covered the entire extent of territory lying between its eastern door at the Hudson and its western door at the Genesee. The Mohawk tended the eastern door, the Seneca the western. The hallway, running through it east and west, was the Mohawk River, another geographical symbol. The home fire of the communal house burned symbolically near its center, near what is now Syracuse, and was tended by the Onondaga. Flanking it were the seats of the Oneida and the Cayuga, near the north and south walls, respectively. As the hallway was the passage for the coming in and going out of the families and nations, so an imaginary line running athwart the middle of the Long House separated it into eastern and western halves. It divided the people of the tribe as well as the nations of the confederacy into "sides," working in part independently, in part reciprocally. In this dual division we see the phratry, or moiety, of clans, whose origin has provoked so much discussion among sociologists.

These parallels constitute a three-sided symbol: the topography of the homeland of the Long House league, with a floor terrain of some two hundred miles; the long house in which they dwelt; and the spirit of cohesion that bound them together in amity as related families coinhabiting a compartment house, each pursuing its own affairs. Always we have the symbols of practice and the practice of symbols, a rubric of Indian culture in the east.

Thus the Five Nations of the Iroquois seat themselves and function in the Long House council to this day. Each has its social privileges and its responsibilities. Each has popular representation in matters debated around its central fire. Each family-nation has its own council fire and its own figurative Long House. The Iroquois envisioned the thirteen original American colonies as confederated in a manner parallel with their own league, and referred to them as the Thirteen Fires.

Thus the League of the Iroquois was an alliance conceived among aboriginal nations which, though culturally related and speaking languages fundamentally similar but differing in vocabulary and idiom, had recurrently been in conflict. The league brought them out of conflict into peace. Then came the French, the Dutch, and the English, and the doom of the league was sealed, its desired results nullified. Here was an alliance binding together five distinct nations, based upon an orally transmitted constitution. It had no inscribed statutes, no taxes or levies, no *gendarmerie,* no hireling politicians. We hear, however, of tribute exacted of subjugated tribes. Tribute, as the Iroquois took it, consisted of stipulated sums of wampum demanded of the Algonkian tribes on the Atlantic Coast who produced it; and wampum was not an item of money, cash, or currency in native economy before the coming of Europeans to the Hudson Valley. Its function was that of a symbol, valuable in a spiritual sense and capable of serving the purposes of mnemonic record making. Thus the wampum tribute we read so much about would seem to be a measure pressed upon subjugated smaller tribes in the shell-bearing coastal regions, requiring them to furnish the wampum the Iroquois needed in the score of ceremonial uses they had developed for it.

We may close this summary with the statement that the League of the Five Nations was the political outgrowth of a civilization of a distinct order, and that enthusiastic authorities have been lavish in their praise of its principles of representative government. Wissler writes: "Students of politics and government have found much to admire in the working of the league. There is some historical evidence that knowledge of the league influenced the colonies in their first efforts to form a confederacy and later to write a constitution."

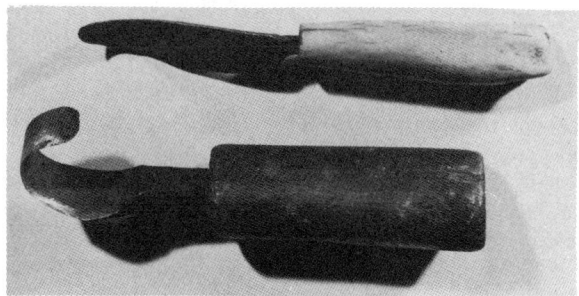

CROOKED KNIVES

Crooked knives are a characteristic tool of eastern Indians and are frequently made from old files, hafted to handles of wood or bone. Such knives are used in carving of wooden objects, preparation of basketry splints and numerous other household tasks. They are held in the hand with the thumb downward toward the blade. These specimens are shorter than most of those encountered from neighboring tribes.

2118. Wooden handle: Six Nations Reserve, 1916-18. M. G. Chandler. 2117. Antler handle. As above.

SMALL MEDICINE BOWL AND HUSKING PEG

The small flat bottomed bowl is typical of Iroquoian medicine bowls. The husking peg is unusual though not unique in that it is of bone, wooden ones being typical among Canadian Iroquois. Bone pegs are characteristic of Central New York and Connecticut.

Bowl: 1913. Oneida Reserve, Wisconsin, 1920. *Peg*: 1912. Six Nations Reserve, 1918. Both M. G. Chandler, donated by Joseph H. Hunter.

Economic and Ecologic Aspects of Iroquois Culture

As economists and agronomists the Iroquois have been successful in raising their food resources to not less than two hundred specific items of diet. This would be a rough estimate of the plant foods listed by two able students, A. C. Parker (1910) and F. W. Waugh (1916), who have each published a monograph on Iroquois foods. This estimate does not include animal resources. Waugh, who admits his list to be incomplete, gives over one hundred recipes for foods prepared from plant forms. By comparison, a casual computation of the recipes reached in modern cookbooks might yield three thousand. However, Europeans have drawn food items from the entire world and Indian food *régimes* are ecologically determined.

Culture statisticians give the Indians a high rating in the ratio of food discoveries between the Old and New World peoples. It is even more to the point to realize that in the modern Euro-American total the actual number of nutritive contributions made to the larder of the country by the Indians is very high. The entire group of foods made from Indian corn, or maize, comes from the native Central American agronomic background, which evolved the corn plant and its products from wild grass ancestors.

The part played by the Iroquois in the agricultural advances of North American aborigines was not that of originators but of carriers who transmitted the maize complex from some southern locale to the Great Lakes and St. Lawrence region. It follows that the maize industry and all its related developments were introduced to the Algonkian-speaking peoples of the east and northeast through Iroquoian associations.

To the Iroquois the three primary sources of nourishment are corn (maize), beans, and squashes. These foods they regard as bestowed upon them by the Creator as sacred gifts; hence they are known as "supporters of life." Far from being profaned by abuse in any manner whatever, especially by waste, these foods play a prominent part in ritual imbued with the spirit of reverence and gratitude. In this sense it may be said that they are worshipped, since they are regarded as a direct means of communication with the elemental spirit, the Creator.

A survey of Iroquois horticultural achievements shows that some 15 to 17 distinct varieties of maize were produced in the course of cultivation from the wild plant ancestor, and that they produced also some 60 varieties of beans (Parker, 1910, listed 10 or more) and about 8 native squashes. We need not name here the 34 wild fruits, 11 nuts, 38 varieties of leaf, stem, and bark substances, 12 varieties of edible roots, and 6 fungi pressed into service to extend the food list without requiring cultivation. There are besides 12 beverages (not to mention pure water) and 11 infusions of parts of plants employed as occasional drinks. Maple sap is the sweetener for all. Salt was but little used with foods in former times.

It is impossible to state accurately the number of animals yielding food to the Iroquois, since no adequate identification of the fish and birds contributing to the food supply has been undertaken. Waugh lists 22 animals, 6 insects, and 4 molluscs made use of in some way. A complete survey, with the uses of the specific forms given, would evidently make a handsome showing for the various Iroquois subdivisions. A rapidly developing interest in native American resources

SENECA SALT BOTTLE
OF CORN HUSK
3004. Cattaraugus Reservation, New York, 1920. A. G. Heath. Height 4 inches, without stopper.

39

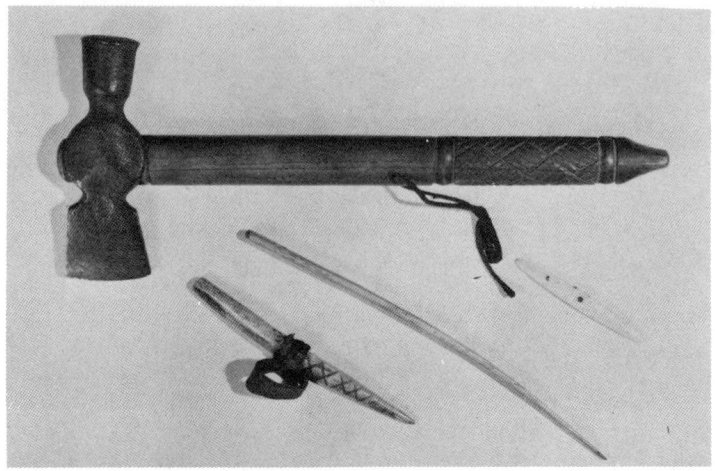

AXE, NEEDLES AND PEG

The iron headed hand axe has a handle drilled as a pipe stem but since the head has no bowl, the union of the two must be considered secondary.

The smaller objects are a wooden mat needle (lower middle), a snow-shoe needle of bone (lower right) and a bone corn husking peg (lower left).

Axe: 2112. *Mat needle*: 2115. *Snow-shoe needle*: 2116. *Husking peg*: 1912. All Six Nations Reserve, 1916-18. M. G. Chandler.

of nutrition as well as medicine is leading attention in this direction.

As farmers the Iroquois were successful adventurers who built a tradition in the northeast for their seminomadic native neighbors and for the hosts of blond invaders from the Old World. Modern American agriculture owes much to the aborigines. The direct contagion of culture in respect to exploitation of native food resources came to the first colonists, as we now know, from the Algonkian-speaking tribes of New England in the early seventeenth century. This statement applies primarily to the cultivation of maize and its nutritional associates—not to mention tobacco. While acculturation was progressing among the natives their long-evolved culture of plants, medicinal as well as edible, was effectively adding to the

HURON SNOWSHOE WEB SPACER

This tool, fashioned from the canon bone of a caribou, is employed to regulate the size of the web openings in snowshoes. After the weaving is complete but while the babiche is yet soft this bone is quickly pushed part way through the webbing to make the spaces even.

3190. Indian Lorette, Quebec. F. G. Speck.

40

larder and the wealth of the Europeans. An extensive native vocabulary went with this plant culture. A review of the terms in the local
vernaculars of America which are distinctly words for foods derived
from native speech, Algonkian in particular, would answer a much-
discussed question concerning the degree of indigenous food adoption by early American colonists. Curiously, neither the names nor
the tastes for these foods have altered.

Kroeber has shown that the length of the growing season and
precipitation are factors responsible in part for the intensity of
agriculture among the Iroquois. In *Cultural and Natural Areas of
Native North America* (University of California Press, 1939) he
reproduces from R. J. Russell's *Dry Climates of the United States*
a map showing "the areas in which a growing season of at least 120
and 100 days, respectively, can be counted on in four years out of
five." Within the eastern bounds of the map lie the territories of
the Huron and Iroquois below the northern limits of the farming
area of the Great Lakes and upper St. Lawrence districts which
could reasonably count on 120 days for maize to grow. Kroeber
writes: "These are all districts in which culture flourished, or population was dense, in comparison with immediately adjacent districts.
By the location of settlements in specially favored spots, it was
probably possible in this area to reduce the expectability of a loss of
crop through frost from two years in ten to one or less. It is clear
that, as among the Pueblos, an agriculture based on tropical plants
had here been pushed to its northern limit of potentiality, at any
rate as an agriculture important and not ancillary to existence. On
the other hand, the adjustment was as stable as it was nice, indicat-
ing the firmness of the attachment of the cultures in question to
their farming basis." In these observations he was considering
ecology incidentally rather than systematically. The Iroquoian
"somewhat greater emphasis on farming than elsewhere in the same
latitudes" he attributes to a somewhat longer and surer growing
season.

As already noted, the elements of native agriculture in eastern
North America emanated from the semitropical latitudes of the
continent. The migration of cultivable plant forms that furnished
nutrition sources to the northern and eastern regions took place
through human agency. Somewhere to the south and west of their
historic seats the Iroquois had become farmers through acquisition
of seed maize, squashes, gourds, beans, and tobacco. Kroeber sug-
gests that they may even be "fragmentary remnants from the Mound
Builder days of heavier population and quasi-states. If there were
such days, and it seems there were, it may well have been the
introduction of agriculture that made their state system possible."
Goldenweiser (1922, 1937) emphasizes that the Iroquois were agri-

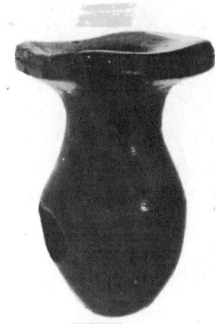

STONE PIPE BOWL

The well marked shape of an Iroquoian pot makes the tobacco pipe bowl referable to the Iroquois.

2196. Reported to have been found near Greenville, Ohio. M. G. Chandler.

culturists first and foremost; their "agricultural activities stood in the very centre of the social and ceremonial life of these tribes and deeply affected their mythological ideas," he writes in his *Anthropology* (1937). Wissler (1940) gives less prominence to Iroquois agricultural achievements than to their militancy, but he depends for his data upon archival sources and not upon impressions gained through his own field work among the people.

The tools and utensils of farming form a large part of the equipment of every Iroquois community and are so represented in museums in so far as they show evidence of native thought or use of native material. Iroquois field tools are made of simple materials and are simple in construction, but they are efficient in the service required of them. The pre-European digging and planting sticks with blades of antler or bone, recorded in chronicles, have long been obsolete and have been replaced by implements of forged

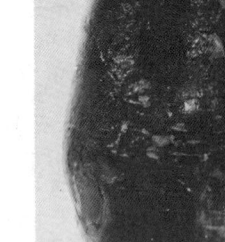

IROQUOIAN POT
910. Wolf Site, Macomb County, Michigan, 1938.
Gwynn Cushman, collector and donor.
Height 20½ inches.

iron. Little remains of the native economy beyond the food substances themselves, methods of storing and preserving them, and, with considerable fidelity to the past, methods of preparation, which most Indians heartily prefer to the cooking rules of the whites.

Iroquois utensils employed in food economy serve purposes ranging from the handling of the harvest to the handling of victuals. Those known to ethnology include objects made of bone, wood, bark, and fiber. Stone utensils are but hazy memories and clay utilization has long been obsolete. European trade materials have supervened.

PESTLE

Double ended pestles are used for pounding dried corn in mortars made of a hollowed section of log. Iroquois pestles are commonly more bulging than those from neighboring Algonkian tribes.

2159. New York State Seneca, 1935. M. G. Chandler. Length 40 inches.

Articles include corn-husking pegs or pins of wood and bone, deer-jaw scrapers for shelling corn from the cob, upright log mortars with double-end wooden pestles for crushing corn into meal, wooden pot stirrers and ladles, wooden eating and feasting bowls, individual wooden spoons, and wooden cups, some with toggle for attachment to the belt. Still remembered but now passed out of general use are box-turtle shell cups, elm-bark hide scrapers, and flat stone anvils with hand stone mullers for crushing nuts and medicinal roots.

The Iroquois series of containers for foods and the like includes a wide range of baskets of varied form and size made of splints of black ash, *Fraxinus nigra* Marsh, and elm-bark pails, trays, dishes, bowls, and spoons. The use of elm bark in Iroquois industry has an ecological significance we cannot overlook. Cayuga tradition states that elm-bark containers antedate those of woven splints. If a chart showing the distribution of the elms of North America is consulted it will be seen that the Huron and Iroquois occupied territory abounding in this culturally valuable tree. It provided them with material for house building, canoe making, and container construction to an extent little realized by those who have given attention to native crafts and their functions as determined by environment.

As published material and museum collections show, the Iroquois were addicted to the use of elm bark as much as the Algonkian north of them and beyond the limits of abundant elm growth were addicted to the use of birch bark, *Betula alba* var. *papyrifera*

43

ELM-BARK TRAY AND CORN SIFTER

The Iroquois made many vessels of elm-bark. This tray, edged with hickory splints and loop stitched with bark fibers, is of the type principally used in the preparation of corn-bread and other foods.

The corn sifter, or hominy strainer basket of splints, has an open checker-weave bottom. Such baskets are still used by the Iroquois from Wisconsin to New York State.

Tray: 2127. Grand River Reserve, 1917. M. G. Chandler. *Sifter*: 2160. Same, 1935.

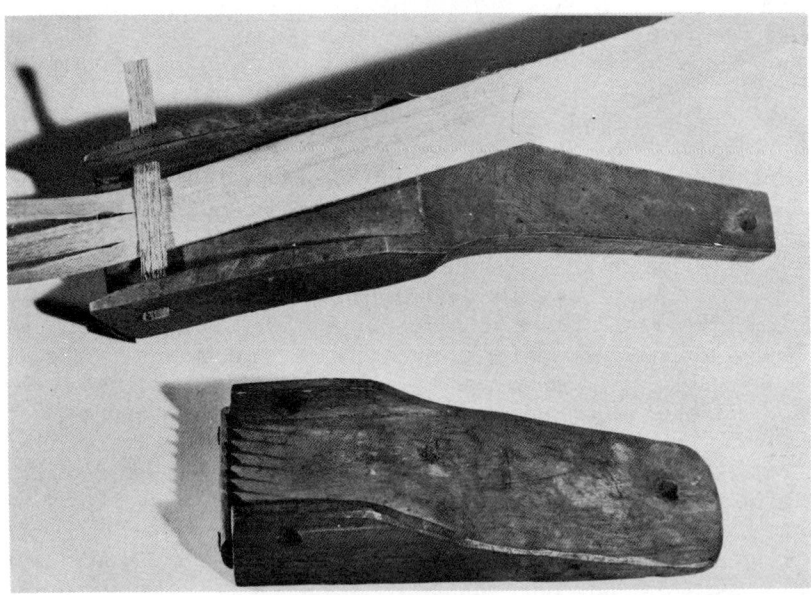

BASKET GAUGES

Basket gauges were adopted or developed in recent times to divide the wood splints into strips of uniform width. The teeth are made of old razor blades or other sharp bits of metal.

Above: 2109. Six Nations Reserve, 1916-18. M. G. Chandler. *Below*: 1621. Oneidas near St. Thomas, Ontario, 1922. M. G. Chandler.

(Marsh). The Central Algonkian people of the same latitude as the Iroquois employ elm bark as they do. Southward its use fades into insignificance. There is therefore a lateral zone of cultural use of elm bark extending from the Great Lakes drainage area to the upper St. Lawrence, and sharply defined from the birch-bark area in the coniferous belt northward. The characteristics of the construction and utilization of these materials by Iroquois and Algonkian are strikingly similar, and there may be a historical problem lurking beneath the surface which will be revealed in a study of

MOOSE-HAIR DECORATED BIRCH-BARK

Great skill was shown by the Indian women who in past years made thousands of such items for the whites as these dyed moose-hair and sweet grass decorated bark objects. It is presumed that work of this type was never done until steel needles were available to the Indians and the convents taught the Indian girls the technique of such embroidery. This group is presumably of Huron workmanship of about 1900 and earlier.

Cigar case: 2133. Chicago, 1926. *Napkin ring with cloth*: 2128. Niagara Falls, N. Y., 1923. *Turkey tail fan holder*: 2132. Auburn, N. Y., 1930. *Trinket box*: 2131. Auburn, N. Y., 1931. All M. G. Chandler.

elm-bark techniques now under contemplation. The ornamental properties of the birch-bark industry are not shared by manufactures in bark of elm, and accordingly aesthetic development does not have a part in the latter as it does in the former.

In studying the Iroquois utensils of agriculture and food making exhibited in the Institute we may consider the statement of Kroeber, who likes to view phenomena in a broad span of intercultural relationships over the continent: "In material culture there were Iroquoian specializations, none of a high order, in pottery, pipes, house types and so forth." The ethnologist primarily concerned with eastern cultures can but accept his decision.

45

Iroquois Arts and Crafts

Various monographs that approach the culture of the Iroquois in a highly generalized fashion include classifications of the crafts, industries, constructions, and utensils employed by the Iroquois in producing the commodities of material existence. Usually the manufactured objects noted in these categories are those collected by the writers of such essays for museum exhibits and for illustration of published reports which describe them in cursory paragraphs, without details of construction, preparation of raw material, or patterning. In other words, they are not technological studies. In using them the student may rely upon some firsthand and, for the time,

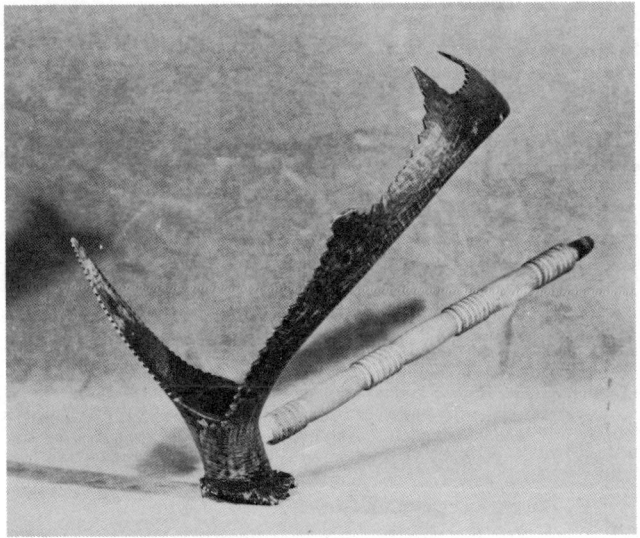

ANTLER PIPE

The bowl of this strange pipe is lined with lead. That it once was decorated with dangles is indicated by perforations along the tine. The stem is restored. Of a similar pipe figured by Beauchamp in 1902, that author wrote: "Fig. 159 is a very fine example of a pipe made from a large antler, which belongs to the writer, and which is probably a little over a century old. It retains the metallic lining in the bowl, without which no pipe of this material could be used. Its history is a little obscure, but it belonged to an early Onondaga pioneer, and was probably made by an Indian of that county. All the prongs but the basal have been cut off, and the bowl is in the cavity between that and the main branch. The carved lines have been filled with red or blue paint, and the holes and some other parts are edged with red. There are numerous perforations, as may be seen. The antler was split from the tip down to the bowl, and the unpolished side painted with Indian red. The stem is made of some light wood, with five encircling bosses, inserted in the stem hole at one end, and tied with buckskin near the other. The antler was an extremely large one of the Virginia deer. It is a very fine article, and probably absolutely unique."

1803. J. S. Johnston. Presented from the Stearns Collection by the Detroit Institute of Arts.

first-rate sources—Morgan, Beauchamp, and Parker among them. In a secondary source treatment of Iroquois economics Stites (1905) outlines the material culture of the people and makes brief mention of their crafts and industries.

It is, however, to Parker (1910) and Waugh (1916) that we turn for topical discussion with adequate illustrations of historic Iroquois commodities and utensils of farming, hunting, fishing, transportation, and food preparation and preservation. The association of native manufactures with food-procuring activities is so close that treatment of one almost covers the other.

Viewing Iroquois crafts and industries from a comparative standpoint, several authorities have expressed the opinion that the Iroquois have not been remarkable in the development of material things. In the judgment of Kroeber (1939) "there were Iroquoian specializations, none of a high order, in pottery, pipes, house types, and so forth." Douglas and d'Harnoncourt (1941, p. 154) consider "Algonkian crafts to be more highly developed than those of the Iroquois," and judge Iroquois crafts as striving for "simple practicability more than for dramatic effect." Even Parker (1927) does not accord the Iroquois a high type of material culture.

Nevertheless, it appears that the exceptional art qualities of Iroquois effigy pipe and ceramic forms, and even perhaps of the bone and antler combs, have been overlooked. These forms are abundantly represented in New York State in collections of the Rochester Museum, the Jefferson County Historical Society in Watertown, and in private collections in Cayuga and Jefferson counties of which Mr. Edmund S. Carpenter has informed me. Murdock (1938, p. 300), in a synopsis of Iroquois culture viewed from a wide comparative angle, refers to the pipes as displaying "great aesthetic freedom and originality" in ornamentation; he adds, with gusto, "they are, indeed, the finest aboriginal pipes north of Mexico."

Iroquoian industry in materials of stone, bone, antler, and clay, recovered from sites of pre- and post-contact eras, has long exerted a strong appeal upon American archaeologists. Parker's extensive contributions are outstanding through the period from 1910 to the present. Problems of cultural sequence and chronology in the perspective of Iroquois history in relation to other horizons, or aspects, in the northeast are fraught with complexities. Some of these problems are now on the way to clarification by W. A. Ritchie.

The culture sequence proposed by Ritchie (1938) relates to New York State; it is not final or complete and is subject to alteration. It begins with an archaic pattern of culture, quite possibly of Algonkian affinity, then follows a northeastern woodland phase-pattern which develops an aspect bearing the name "Owasco." Finally the Iroquois aspect emerges. This aspect Ritchie dates from

47

about 1300. The change in culture due to white invasion he dates from the beginning of historic times in New York: which leads us into the sphere of culture treated in the present essay.

While the industrial background of Iroquois culture has not yet been treated as a whole by an ethnographer, there are those who have dealt with one or another technique as of particular concern to the social or political life of the group or in their religious ceremonials. Thus Beauchamp examined the history and manner of making wampum; Fenton has told and shown how masks were made, and Lismer has done the same for basket making among the Seneca, and Orchard for porcupine-quill work in Iroquois decoration. Silver working in the post-contact era of Iroquois technology has claimed attention from its amateurs, Converse, Beauchamp, Harrington, Parker, and Gillingham.* Morgan wrote on Iroquois fabrics, Barbeau (1928?) found an interest in the history and manufacture of Iroquois (Huron, derived from Canadian-French) sash weaving, and the writer once found inspiration for a technical article in Huron moose-hair embroidery (Speck, 1911).

ONEIDA WOMEN'S
BUCKSKIN MOCCASINS
In cold weather the side flaps are
turned up and bound to the leggings.
2139. Oneida Reserve, Wisconsin,
1925. M. G. Chandler.

*This subject has been profusely treated. Gillingham finds that between 1758 and 1762 alone 8300 silver ornaments were made for Indians by Philadelphia silversmiths.

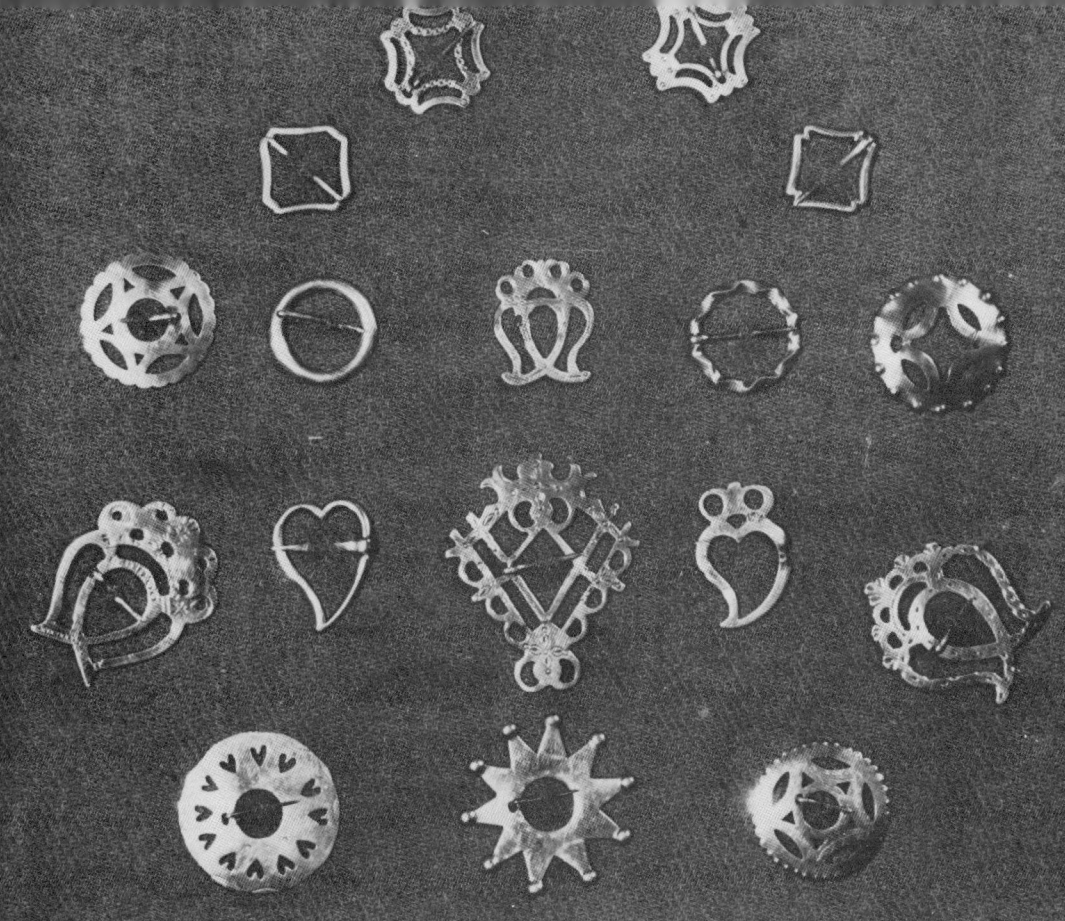

Silver came to the Iroquois with such other trade goods as broadcloth, beads, and woven sashes, but in time some of the Iroquois took up the craft of silversmithing, usually copying the work of Montreal and other silversmiths engaged in the manufacture of Indian trade goods. There is no means of knowing which, if any, of the silver brooches in the Institute collection were Indian made, but the single crowned heart (No. 13 in progressive count) in the group bears the hallmark of Robert Cruickshanks of Montreal, and may be ruled out.
2148. Six Nations Reserve, 1918-1923. M. G. Chandler.

Summing up, however, source material exists in abundance for a monograph on Iroquois technology which has not yet been undertaken.

One of the tasks Morgan set for himself in 1849 was to collect specimens of Iroquois handicrafts and manufactures for the New York Historical and Antiquarian Collection. He classified these objects into eighty-three distinct classes. It is significant that after the lapse of almost a century most of them could be duplicated among the same Indians. At the time of writing Morgan (1850) did

ONEIDA COSTUME DOLL
The doll, with body of corn-husk, wears a costume of the period of 1820-60 but is of more recent make.
1627. Near Appleton, Wisconsin, 1925. M. G. Chandler.

not attribute to the art and craft knowledge of the Indians the tena-cious quality it seems to possess. As he wrote, the primitive fabrics had mostly passed away by his time, and with them many of their original inventions. "They have laid aside their deerskin apparel," Morgan continues, "and substituted materials, in fact, of our own manufacture . . . the deerskin has been laid aside for the broad-cloth, the bearskin blanket for the woolen, and the porcupine quill for the bead."

Thus one of the thresholds of acculturation had evidently been crossed over by 1820, and the Iroquois were in an era of transition in material culture. The change from leather to trade cloth material in the garb of the Iroquois took place at about the close of the eighteenth century, as Morgan assumed.* He described the habiliments of the people of his time and their transition from the preceding period.

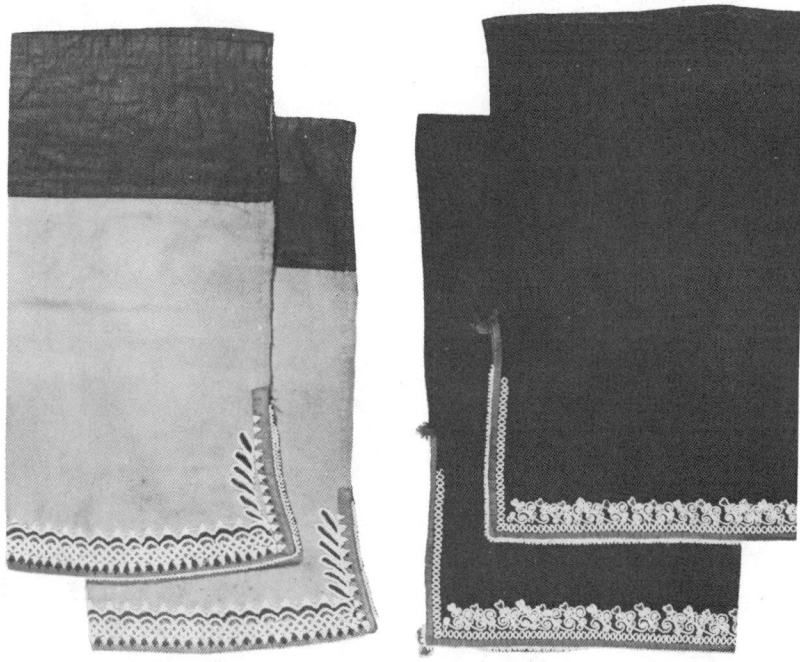

WOMEN'S LEGGINGS

These beaded broadcloth leggings were tied by garters below the knee and hung to touch the moccasin tops. The pair on the left is on red broadcloth, that on the right on black. They are of the style and materials of the early 19th century.

Left: 1628. Cayuga. Caledonia, Ontario, 1922. M. G. Chandler. *Right:* 2243. Brantford, Ontario, 1922. M. G. Chandler.

The adoption of foreign-made glass beads marked the vanishing point of porcupine-quill embroidery techniques, while design patterning evidently temporarily expanded and widened its range as a result of the change. Examples of Iroquois clothing and personal accessories preserved in museum collections seldom date from a period earlier than this transitional era. In such collections we behold the type forms of men's leggings, kilts, and shirts, women's

---

*No better phrasing of the emphasis of change could be found than the words of Henry Beston (1942, p. 242): "The Stone Age Iroquoian primitive had in a scant hundred years crossed the astronomical abyss between the Neolithic and the Age of Louis Quinze."

51

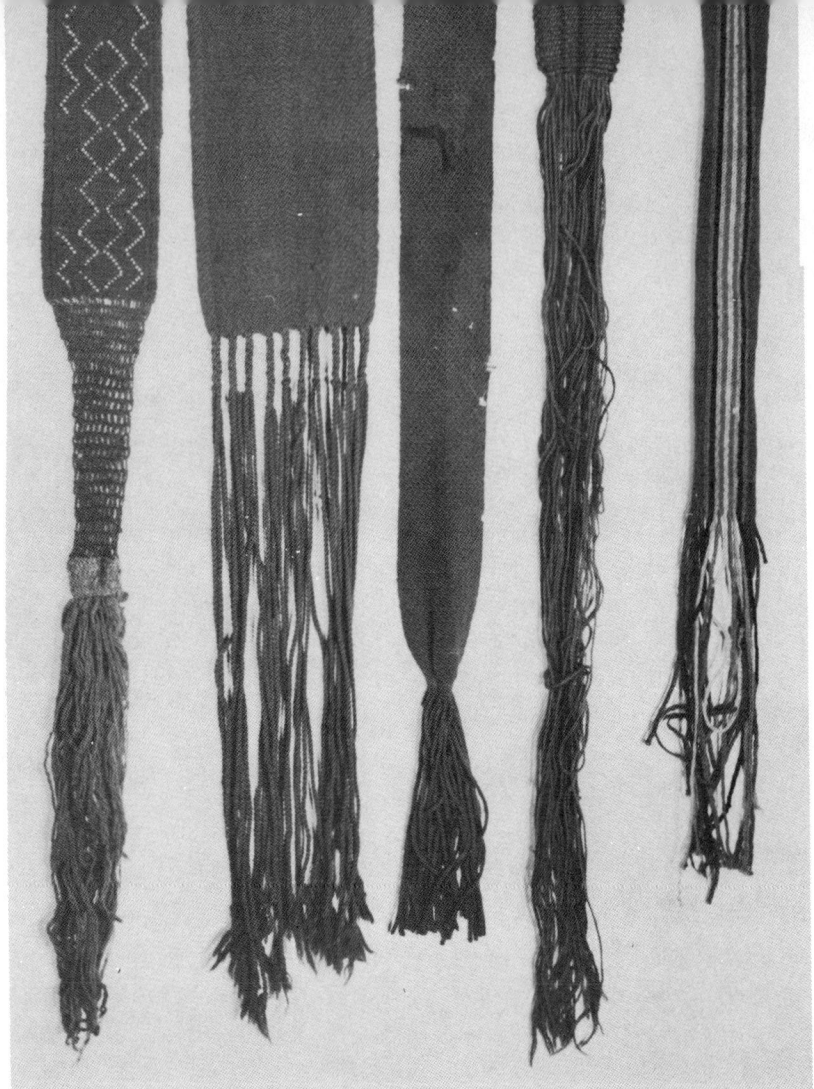

IROQUOIS SASHES

The sash or belt, worn by men, was a highly prized article of costume. Sometimes it was worn over the left shoulder and around the waist, other times around the waist only. It served to hold in the shirt and as a ring into which could be tucked the tobacco pouch, knife, cup, and other personal possessions.

Sashes were sometimes made by finger weaving; occasionally with beads interwoven, sometimes on a heddle loom, later crocheting and by machine. Many came into the Iroquois country by trade and it cannot be known whether any in this group are of Indian manufacture.

The sashes may be described left to right as follows: Red wool with white beads strung in open spaces. Knitted with crochetted ends—length 92 inches, width 3½ inches. Red wool, loomed (?)—length 108 inches, width 5½. Red wool, Hudson Bay trade type; loomed (?)—length 98 inches, width 3. Red and blue, possibly finger woven—length 96 inches, width 3. Red with stripes in blue, black, yellow, red, and white; knitted—length 90 inches, width 3½.

2151, 2153, 2152, 2156, 2155. All Six Nations Reserve, 1918. M. G. Chandler.

PLAITED GARTER

Wool garters were finger woven in the same technique as were many large sashes. This pair is red with blue.

2154. Six Nations Reserve, 1918. M. G. Chandler.

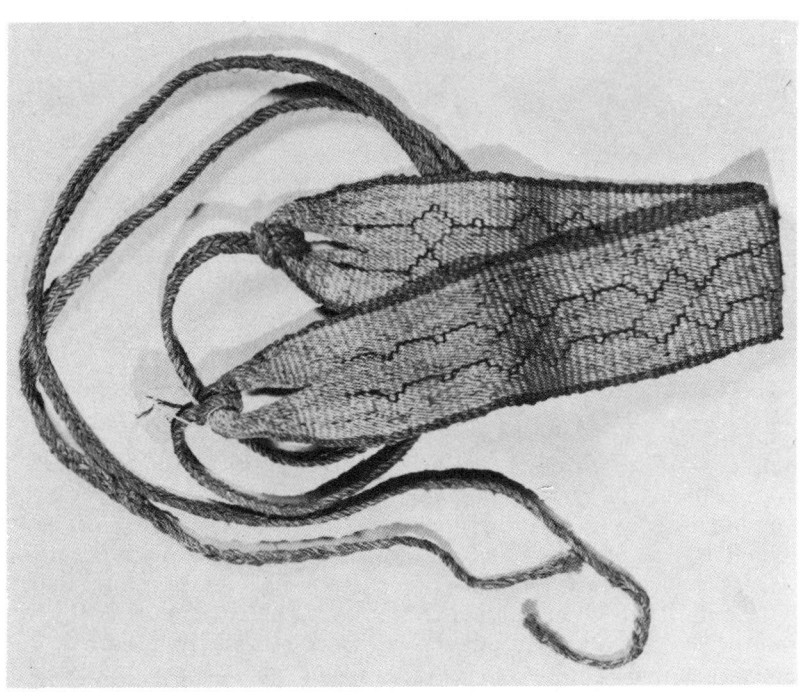

CAYUGA BURDEN STRAP

Such burden straps or tump lines were commonly used, worn across the forehead and lashed to a litter borne on the back by Indian women. The straps were commonly of basswood bark fiber or leather, sometimes decorated with moosehair. This specimen is of nettle fiber, decorated with green and red yarn. It is of typical Delaware type and may be considered as probably from that Algonkian tribe living among the Iroquois along the Grand River.

1629. Caledonia, Ontario, 1922. M. G. Chandler. Length 92 inches, width 2¾.

blankets for head and shoulders, waists, overdresses, and skirts, in black, red, and dark blue broadcloth and calico. Their border patterns of design in white beaded line work carry over the art tradition of the preceding century, with efflorescences prompted by an appreciation of the art devices of colonial French and English artists. How many ethnologists, imbued with the sentiments of antiquarians, have lamented the encroachments of European decorative figures upon the imaginary "pure" art horizon of pre-contact times. However, examined and judged objectively, Iroquois art of the material transition era shows expansion rather than degeneration under the impetus of new supply material, sewing mediums, and designs to imitate.

A still lightly touched field of investigation lies in full view at the present time. Assuming that the prehistoric Iroquoian people

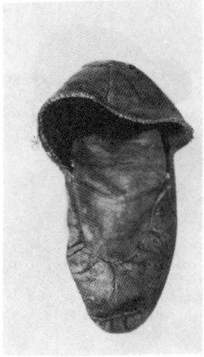

BULL-NOSE MOCCASIN

The common puckered moccasin predominates among the Iroquois but there is also made a type with a T-shaped seam on the toe which the Huron call the Bull-Nose. The moccasin illustrated is of heavy buckskin or moosehide, sinew sewn. Side flaps are lost.

2158. Six Nations Reserve. M. G. Chandler.

moving from a warmer to a colder zone of residence were forced to adjust themselves to a changed environment by increasing the amount of winter clothing they wore, we look for a source from which the needed garment forms were derived. The survey may halt at the northern boundary of the Iroquois migration line; that is, where the Laurentian-plateau Algonkian hunters endured the winters in sleeved upper garments, with hoods and head shawls. The general similarity between Iroquois and Algonkian types of clothing in material and decoration cannot be ignored when collections from both groups during the historic period are compared.

It should not be expected that each article of personal raiment of the groups under consideration can be compared, for tribal variations are manifest even within the Algonkian bands. Nevertheless, there is as much to attribute to Algonkian association in types of

54

footwear (tanned skin moccasin and seamless "hock" boot), upper body wear, tailored coating with "Capuchin" hood, and Huron and northern Iroquois protective winter raiment, as far as we know its details, as there is in the use of snowshoes, toboggans, hand sleds, and plank cradleboards, tanning processes, and, in embroidery techniques, of porcupine quills and moose hair.

We discover at this juncture how little is known and recorded of the equipment of the Iroquois as denizens of the northern forest zone where they have lived and roved for over two centuries. Algonkian neighbor influences upon Iroquois life have seldom come in for more than a conjectural thought among ethnologists in treating the eastern area. Glancing for a moment toward the Cherokee, there is no characteristic of their material existence that can be traced to an Algonkian source.

The articles of personal service made of cloth and decorated with beadwork, all of the middle historic period, are listed and illustrated in the Institute collection in forms similar to those so presented by Morgan. They comprise bags, pouches, purses, wall pockets, needlecases, and pincushions ornamented in the art style of the high tide of Iroquois acculturation. The separate objects in the series reveal in their construction characteristics that challenge explanation on the ground of their wider distribution among Algonkian groups of the north and east.

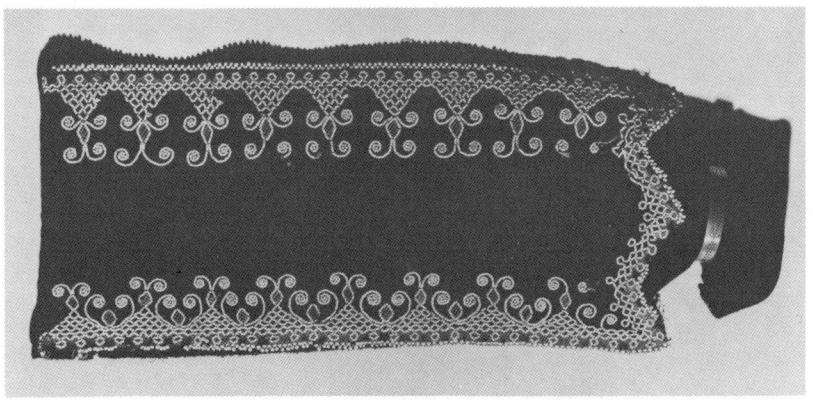

CRADLE BAND AND SILVER BRACELET

These broadcloth bands were wrapped around the infant to hold it in its cradle board. Morgan shows two such in use on one board. The bracelet, of German silver, Indian worked, may have served as a trinket to amuse the child. The beaded decoration is in the familiar double-curve motif. The period of the wrapper is apparently early 19th century.

2149. Grand River Reserve, 1917. M. G. Chandler. Width 5¼ inches; length, beaded section, 11½ inches.

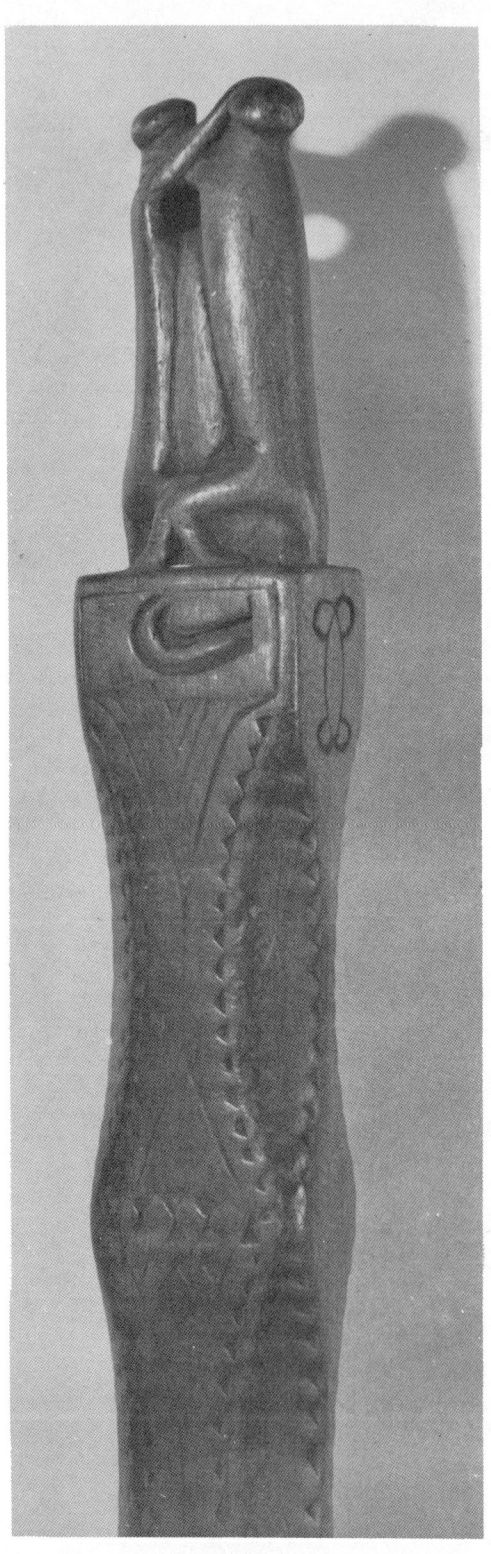

CAYUGA
CORN SOUP STIRRER

Long undecorated corn soup stirrers are common in the long-houses, but this with a pair of otters surmounting its handle is unusual. The indented triangular patterning is produced by tapping a file-end into the wood, and is typical of Delaware woodwork.

1622. Caledonia, Ontario, 1922. M. G. Chandler.

56

Iroquois Decorative Design and Symbolism

That Iroquois art has been so little discussed in literature dealing with native art in aboriginal America cannot be accounted for by sterility of the material or lack of stimulus furnished by problems involved in its development, for material is abundant in the eastern museums from the early period of the nineteenth century. However, specific data about time, place, and maker are lacking, and problems of derivation and art content are as unsettled as they were in Morgan's time.

Lewis H. Morgan was the first investigator to direct attention to the forms and techniques of decoration observed on Iroquois costumes and articles of personal use among the Seneca of New York. When he wrote on the subject in 1849 (Morgan, 1850) acculturation had proceeded so far that he observed that the Indian articles "rather exhibit the application of Indian ingenuity to fabrics of foreign manufacture, as shown in their reduction into use, than originality of invention. . . . Within the past century great changes have been wrought among the descendants of the ancient Iroquois. The primitive fabrics have mostly passed away. . . . The substitution of fabrics of more skillful hands, has led to the gradual disuse of many of their simple arts." Morgan's thirty-page report on the collections made for the New York Historical and Antiquarian Society was illustrated with seventeen color plates showing Iroquois designs in quillwork and beadwork. They have become standard reference illustrations of design forms in Iroquois art of the period.

Not until 1910 did art reproduction and discussion of processes, designs, and their symbolism receive notice from the pen of the ethnologist, and then it was Parker who sensed the values of symbols in quill embroidery and later beadwork designs in relation to Iroquois mythology, and offered his findings in several interpretative papers. In a report to the director of the New York State Museum Parker announced that he had given much attention to the decorative art and symbolism of the New York Indians and was holding a manuscript on the subject as a nucleus for further study. In 1913 he published an article on Iroquois tree myths and symbols which, though brief, remains the standard reference on Iroquois decorative patterns and their symbolism.

A little earlier, in 1911, I had produced a short account of Huron moose-hair embroidery, and later, in 1914, a brief treatment of the forms of Iroquois decoration, curvilinear and floristic, as phenomena of art motivation among Algonkian groups of the north and east. The historical possibility of the northern affinities of Iroquois decorative techniques and design figures in relation to Algonkian art characteristics is discussed in a brief report published by the Heye Foundation (Speck, 1925).

Another contributor to the literature on native techniques of decoration is W. C. Orchard, who in 1916 brought out a monograph on the porcupine quillwork of America in which he described and illustrated old Huron and Iroquois specimens in the collections of the Museum of the American Indian. Passing attention is given to the technical aspects of Iroquois art in beadwork in the same author's monograph of 1929. In neither, however, does his treatment include design analysis.

Where may search be directed to trace the source from which northern Iroquois and Huron formal elements in art may have arisen? Could they have been transmitted to historic Iroquoian-speaking groups from a common ancestral vicinage beyond the Appalachians, coincident with the common speech? Could they have been evolved out of a richly endowed art genius by the Iroquois people in the period of settled residence in the northeast? Could they have been taken over by the Iroquois during this period from the art traditions of Algonkian predecessors in the northeastern woodlands?

So far as the question of an art heritage common to the linguistic stock is concerned the answer would rest with the Cherokee. However, since the Cherokee were not and are not producers of embroidery figures, either in porcupine quills or beads, there exists no series of decorated articles of clothing or domestic wares to afford a basis of comparison. Cherokee clothing, never profuse in type, developed in historic times from printed cotton cloth imported into the southern Appalachians by English and French traders. The small seed beads used in sewed-on decorative embroidery by Indians throughout the north and west did not become an element of trade in the southeastern highlands. Except for the decorative designs incised or impressed by a paddle upon the outer walls of pottery vessels and the geometrical figures in color woven into the sides of diagonal twill cane and oak splint baskets, the Cherokee exhibit no field of representative or symbolic art. This fact is as strange as it is striking when one considers the cultural achievements of the Cherokee. The complete disparity between the designs of the two peoples in their appropriate fields of decoration leaves no tangible ground for supposing that their art forms had a common source within the historic period.

An alternative explanation is that the Iroquois developed their own art forms. One might ponder long upon the nature of the evidence of such self-development in any ethnic environment. However, no historical perspectives can be conjured up to warrant the

RIBBON APPLIQUE AND BEAD WORK ON BLACK BROADCLOTH
WITH UNIVERSE SYMBOLS

This may have been a skirt border or a cradle-board wrapper. It would seem to
date to the early 19th century.

2150. Six Nations Reserve, 1918. M. G. Chandler.

conclusion that the birth and growth of the kind of decorative phenomena the Iroquois of the northeast present were limited to their own immediate sphere of culture. Examination of embroidery techniques, the design figures produced, and the symbolism associated with them shows that Iroquois art characteristics line up with those of Algonkian groups over a wide zone north, east, and west of the Great Lakes region. Accordingly, it would appear to be a mistake to seek for an art impulse latent within the cultural impulse of the Iroquois. In such instances of a wide diffusion of art types a decision as to its birthplace may better be held in abeyance until historical evidence is available.

Another likelihood arises if we concede that the Iroquois reached the eastern Great Lakes region by migration, that the premigration sources of their art style cannot be traced backward satisfactorily, and that this style is part of an art complex unbroken in extent over the zone into which the migration entered. That is, the likelihood that the art of the Iroquois, as we know it ethnologically, is one of the aspects of culture transmitted to them by association with Algonkian predecessors in the northeast. Such an explanation is in line with the ideas of students of the Iroquois, who attribute certain other elements of their culturation to a similar source.

Other opinions concerning the origin of designs in the northwestern area should not be overlooked. Barbeau in 1928 gave it as his opinion that these designs were derived from French influence commencing in the mid-seventeenth century in convent circles in Quebec. More recently Quimby has discerned a possible connection

59

between northern Algonkian art and the prehistoric Hopewell culture of Ohio. In a letter (1943) addressed to me he expresses the belief that "the double-curve motif occurs in the Hopewell. If this is so then the double-curve is prehistoric, which is in accord with suggestions made by you in 1914."

Though there is as yet no adequate study of Iroquois art, some features of design in the Iroquois material in museums are distinct enough to warrant comparisons with Algonkian design figures.

The characteristic Algonkian double-curve motive has been the subject of sufficient definition, analysis, and historical discussion to need no introduction to readers who have pursued this topic. The bisymmetrical double-curve designs are no less prominently displayed in historic Iroquois beadwork and former quillwork than among the northern Algonkian. Some of the Iroquois figures are identical with those of the Algonkian tribes east and north of them. However, it is significant in Iroquois symbolism that the greater number of the Iroquois designs exhibit the curves turning outward instead of inward.

Parker (1911, p. 48) has reported that the curved line figures are primarily representations of celestial, geographical, and mythical phenomena, such as sky dome, world tree, scroll or helix, sun, and chief's horns. The scrolls themselves denote "horns" of chieftaincy, those curving outward symbolizing a living chief, while the in-curving figures are emblematical of a dead chief. The curve or scroll decorations produced as borders on clothing and bead decorated articles are in general known among the Mohawk as "horned trimming," even by persons who are not now aware of their political symbolism.

The Tuscarora call the scrolls "violets" (literally, "bowing the heads"), and regard them as a sign of good luck. The name is derived from a children's game in which violet blossoms held by children on opposite sides are struck together, and one of the violets is beheaded as a result. The scroll violet is a symbol of the winner in contests, and hence of good luck. The Mohawk of Desderonto call the scrolls "fern heads."

Technically it is not difficult to identify at sight the double curves of the Iroquois as distinguished from those of the Algonkian, for the Iroquois outcurves and series of drooping scrolls or half curves as they appear in the figures are very distinctive. The Iroquois figures are also smaller and finer in line dimensions and have fewer of the interior embellishments so frequent in Algonkian figures.

Iroquois principles of design technique and form are part of a style area extending from the Atlantic and up the St. Lawrence drainage area to and beyond the Great Lakes. There are outlying adjacent zones of conformity in design north and somewhat south

IROQUOIS PURSES

The purses in this collection all show the double curve motif done in fine beads, except for the specimen in the lower right, which has a clearly floral pattern done in large beads. This latter is presumably from the late 19th century; the others from a period before 1870. Such purses were frequently made for sale to whites, and these with pincushions of similar workmanship and design are still commonly encountered.

Upper left: 2144. Small bag of black velvet. Six Nations Reserve, 1918. M. G. Chandler. *Upper right*: 1915. Probably Wyandotte. M. G. Chandler. Presented by Joseph H. Hunter. *Center left*: 2136. Purse, probably Seneca. Cleveland, Ohio, 1927. M. G. Chandler. *Center right*: 1982. History unknown. Presented by Adolph Spohr. *Lower left*: 2137. Bead and ribbon applique on broadcloth, probably Wyandotte. Upper Sandusky, Ohio. M. G. Chandler. *Lower right*: 1795. New Orleans, Louisiana. R. T. Hatt.

and southwest of the major area which are not of direct concern in the present discussion. The symmetrical curved designs of the Iroquois are typical of the decoration of the North American boreal belt—primarily the coniferous forests inhabited by hunting bands for the most part of Algonkian classification.

Some ideas respecting the supposed derivation of Iroquois design patterns from the Algonkian whose habitat in the north they invaded during one of America's historic migrations may be discussed in this connection. The study of decorative art in the northeast, which is evoking increasing interest among ethnologists, now assumes a rôle of considerable historical importance in relation to the whole question of Iroquois-Algonkian relationships. If we make even a casual survey of the types of designs within the range of northern culture just defined we discover that in the decorative patterns of both groups the symmetrical double curve recurs as a design unit. This is the important point, for evidence is well established to show the wide distribution in former times of the Algonkian double-curve decorative figure as far south as southern New England and the Middle Atlantic slope. An inference not to be slighted follows: that Iroquois and Huron art motives and techniques were acquired from Algonkian predecessors in the northeast, or, to put it in another way, that Iroquois migration may have resulted in the imposition of the general art style of the northern area upon that of the newcomers in that area. That this explanation' was the true one the author sensed with equal conviction in 1925, after carrying on field investigations of the distribution of art types among Canadian tribes. (*See* Speck 1914, 1925.)

Here we may remind ourselves that, as Fenton puts it, the eastern Algonkian enemies of the Laurentian Iroquois were descendants of tribes the Iroquois had originally displaced from the St. Lawrence Valley, and that adjustments to the surrounding Algonkian peoples of the northeast had taken place. Such influences, as they had affected one band of Mohawk in Quebec, were discussed by the author in a brief paper published in 1923. Yet historical sources give no clue to the date of any major adjustment to northern ecology or to Algonkian ideas of any sort. The process of adjustment may well have been a gradual cultural hybridization, with intermarriage between the two groups. Indeed, it would seem to presume too much upon credulity to suppose that the influences in art coming from the Algonkian coresidents could be traced back to the Laurentian period or to the Huron period, as early as 1650.

The prehistoric art style of the Iroquois preserved on pottery vessels is based on the incised straight line appearing in angular combinations of groups of parallels, with a moderate degree of elaboration. This style became extinct shortly after the time of discovery.

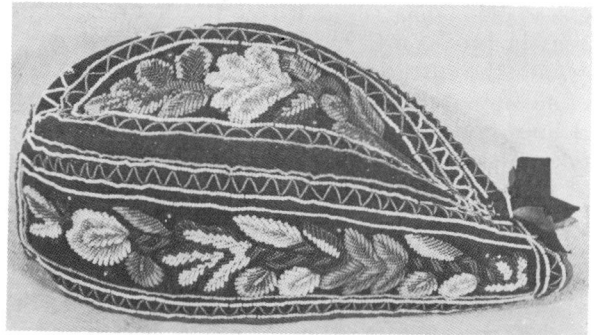

GLENGARRY BONNET

Such caps were common from about 1840 to 1870, and were a direct adaptation of Highlander's headgear. Note that in this period large beads were used and the decorative pattern was distinctly floral and unsymmetrical.

2146. Grand River Reservation, 1918. M. G. Chandler.

HAIR EMBROIDERED MOCCASIN TOPS

Unfinished tops of broadcloth decorated with dyed moosehair. The technique is probably not aboriginal and may have been developed in the convents. These are probably of Huron manufacture and from Indian Lorette near Quebec, where the craft continued until about 1915, (Speck).

Left: 2143. Black broadcloth. Niagara Falls, N. Y., 1923. M. G. Chandler. *Right*: 1199. Red broadcloth. Niagara Falls, 1896. Joseph H. Hunter.

So Douglas (1934) has summarized the matter in his leaflet on design areas in Indian art.

Passing into the historic period of the early eighteenth century, as nearly as can be estimated, the development of art took the form of curved lines grouped around geometrical figures or curved lines in the bilateral symmetrical arrangement already discussed.

The art style of the Iroquois crossed over another threshold of changing phases about the middle of the nineteenth century, when quasi-realistic representations of plants and flowers in beadwork and quillwork on cloth came boldly into vogue. This style affected the art of tribes over the entire Great Lakes area, the northeast quarter of the United States, Canada as far west as the Rockies, and then north to Alaska. Later it even invaded the western plains area. As Douglas observes, "The style is the outgrowth of the meeting of an aboriginal Indian art based on curving lines with the floral style existing in France in the 17th and 18th centuries."

In this epoch of acculturation the symbolism of native art began to lose its hold upon the imagination of the people in the affected zone. Thereafter the surge into favor of the floral patterns, in more or less realistic guise, may be reasonably attributed to the attempt of Indian artists to conform to European ideals of beauty and attractiveness in beaded embroidery as a measure to promote the sale of their work.

This brief summary of conditions should not close without mention of the spread eastward of the real floral figures of later vintage to the Wabanaki tribes of northern New England and the Maritime Provinces of Canada, as well as to the surviving Algonkian groups in southern New England within the last century and a half. Floral beaded figures done after Iroquois models, and often sewed on cloth over patterns cut out of paper with scissors, usurped earlier styles of decoration over an extensive area where the outstanding personalities of Iroquois culture exerted an influence upon tribal traditions.

Ceremonial Properties of the Iroquois

The place of the masked likeness, or prosopic image as classicists prefer to call it, in religious and dramatic art among various peoples of the world is widely known. Oriental and Occidental civilizations, early and late, show an almost universal perception of the mysterious force exerted by masks upon the unstable and sensitive emotions of mankind. Dramatists and romancers in prose and poetry have vied with scientific writers in sounding its uncanny depths. Publications dealing with the multifarious aspects of masking in art and religion in Africa, Asia, the Pacific, and Europe have been produced abundantly, and in the New World the literature has

SENECA BUFFALO TYPE MASK

The buffalo masks usually have horns but their most characteristic features are a pug-nose and a horrible grin exposing formidable teeth. The face is black, the ears of leather. The type is characteristic of the Senecas of Newtown.

1130. Albert G. Heath.

65

CAYUGA FALSE FACE

This old black face with red lips is called *hadu'i* or the Hunchback by the Onondaga, *gagon'hsa* or false face by the Seneca. The mask is consecrated with sacred tobacco bags and annointed with sunflower oil.

3040. Six Nations Reserve, 1943. Robert T. Hatt, from Jerry Aaron, *Sadeganhes,* of Sour Springs Cayuga.

66

mounted from scattering descriptions in bulletins and journals to chapters in treatises on the Eskimo, the tribes of the Northwest Coast, the Southwest, and parts of South America. With but few exceptions, however, the literature concerning American masks and the problems of their history and function has had little bearing upon tribes of the Appalachian or eastern region. Explanations of this neglect are scarcely called for: the region has simply not appealed to the interest of investigators except for a limited group of ethnologists and archeologists of recent schooling.

MASKS

However, our concern is with the Iroquois as makers and users of mask images and perpetuators of the rich lore developed about them, as known for three hundred years of the cultural cycle. Pertinent data assembled from early documents, museum catalogues, and systematic field work have been made available by William Nelson Fenton in a series of essays which serve as the groundwork for further study of masks and masked rituals in the east.

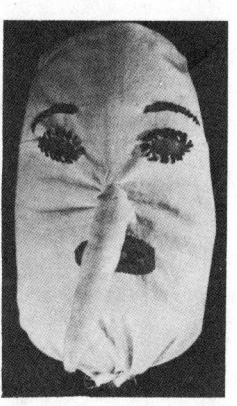

SENECA LONG-NOSE

Cloth long-nose masks are worn to frighten children into obedience. This mask was made by Clara Red Eye. 1824. Allegheny Reservation, 1942. F. G. Speck.

In every collection and exhibit of material, public or private, representing Iroquois culture the mask is outstanding in importance. This prominence is not entirely attributable to the appeal the mask exerts upon the fancy of collectors or admirers of the grotesque. To the Iroquois themselves the masks are important as symbols of spirit forces representing the "environing elements and bodies and many creatures of a teeming fancy" which they look upon as affecting their welfare. Hewitt insisted that masks, or "faces" as the Iroquois generally call them, are really likenesses; a statement Fenton (1940) elaborates by saying they are likenesses "in the sense that they are portraits of mythological beings, and they are not masks for

67

"OLD BROKEN-NOSE"

Iroquois hunters met quasi-human beings in the forests, dreamed of them afterward and carved their faces in living basswood trees. This one represents the first man, Old Broken-nose, whose nose was injured by a moving mountain in a contest of power. His twisted mouth blows hot ashes over the sick in healing rites.

The carving in modern masks such as this is freer, more sophisticated, than in early masks, and reflects the better quality of tools available to the makers. White horse-tail, sheet copper, and red barn paint which decorate this mask are modern substitutes for shorter animal hair, clam shells, and earth pigments.

3754. Made 1937 by Elon Webster, an Onondaga carver of Tonawanda Reservation, New York. William N. Fenton.

the purpose of concealment. The mask itself is only a symbol which operates on the principle of substituting a part for the whole, and the wearer behaves as if he were the supernatural being whom he impersonates. These supernaturals are Wind or Disease Gods of two classes and several varieties, and they are portrayed by wooden or husk faces that are described in the myths, but their human counterparts show a great deal of individual variation."

Fenton summarizes the difficulty confronting ethnologists who, in studying museum collections of Iroquois masks, are forced to rely upon "the lore that has come down through successive curators as to their supposed function." As to this point, it happens that there existed up to 1937 over a dozen accounts and descriptions of the use of Iroquois image masks, some of which were at odds with respect to names and functions. In the face of the rather extensive literature on the subject Fenton urges the need of an adequate monograph on classification of the so-called false faces in terms of the rituals in which they were used, and advocates dependence upon the ideas of the Indians who still use them, as the more trustworthy custodians of tradition. Fenton's several monographs (1937, 1940, 1941, 1942) on the mask phenomena of the Iroquois in general and the Seneca in particular are examples of the prescribed method of approach to the subject. The present author has drawn heavily upon Fenton's *Masked Medicine Societies of the Iroquois,* which covers most of what any ethnological authority could say to date.

Fenton classifies the wooden masks or false faces observed by museum visitors—those "weird human likenesses which mock them from the showcases [and] are actually memorials to generations of nightmares"—under twelve types, as follows: crooked-mouth, straight-lipped, spoon-lipped, hanging-mouth, tongue-protruding, wry-faced and smiling, whistler, divided (red and black), long-nose, horned, animal (pig), blind. To this list the author can add another category, specimens of which he observed and collected among the Cayuga in Canada, namely, the disease-marked visages, and still another, the messenger mask. If one wished to take account of minutiae it would be feasible, according to the same Cayuga sources, to subdivide the wooden faces further according to their red, black, brown, or white coloring and details of featurization. The variations indicated portray distinct spiritual personalties owning separate functions with their own histories as apparitions among the Cayuga.

Besides the wooden false faces there is a series of forms constructed of corn husks by the process of braiding and sewing or twining. The former are widespread among Iroquois mask makers; the latter seem restricted to the Seneca of New York State. Fenton concisely defines the corn husk masks as representing "another class

69

CAYUGA
CORN HUSK MASK

Corn husk masks are worn by members of the doctor's Society of Corn Husk Faces. This well-made plaited false face of the old-man type is consecrated by "sacrifice bags" of native tobacco on the forehead.

1259. Sour Springs, Six Nations Reserve, about 1932. F. G. Speck. It was made by Sayehwas.

of earthbound supernatural beings who formed a pact with mankind and taught them the arts of hunting and agriculture." He does not subdivide them into personage types. Yet among the Canadian Cayuga at least five variant types have been distinguished according to the witness of Long House leaders: eyedropper, cornflower, bisexual face, "disappearing image," which denotes a husk face of normal size with a miniature mask attached to the upper right or left side, and "old man," or chief of the mask company, whose hoary age is symbolized by puffy cheeks, nose, and lips, and wrinkles. The total number of mask creations in stereotype forms and their modifications among the tribes of the league who follow the faith of the ancestors may even exceed two dozen.

In still another category stand the miniature mask images, which form a series corresponding in the delineation of features, in color, and in the material of which they are made with the masks of normal dimensions. Iroquois maskettes, as they have been called, seldom exceed three inches in length. They follow the patterns of the larger images according to the styles prevailing on different reservations and among the tribes comprising the Iroquois group. Their functions are still incompletely known. Even the Indians who possess them have personal reasons for doing so which they do not freely discuss and which may be known only to themselves. The author's information from the Cayuga, for instance, shows some difference of ideas from the data recorded by others among Seneca and Onondaga traditionalists. These small images have concealed assets which are constantly being revealed as secrecy is relaxed and the Indians tell us more about them. Aside from being kept as personal "charms" with a protective power, they serve as substitutes for the large masks worn on the faces of performers in ceremonies when disease spirits are invoked for aid. The lore of the small mask images goes deep and wide beneath the surface of the religious behavior of the Iroquois. Maskettes made of clay and graven in stone have been discovered in earth sites at sundry points in the Atlantic states within and adjacent to the Iroquois territories. They date the existence of these protective talismans to an era before the coming of Europeans.

From examination of many series of Iroquois mask images it would appear, as Fenton concluded after observing over one hundred in various collections, that they range from the main category of seriously respected icons of importance in religious ceremonies to that of tragi-comic works of dramatic art, an example of which is shown among the illustrations.

The idea has been widely held that any people who employ images in any manner in their religious system fall under the classification of idolaters—a word that carries a condemnatory tone. It has been applied to the Iroquois who follow the teachings of the native

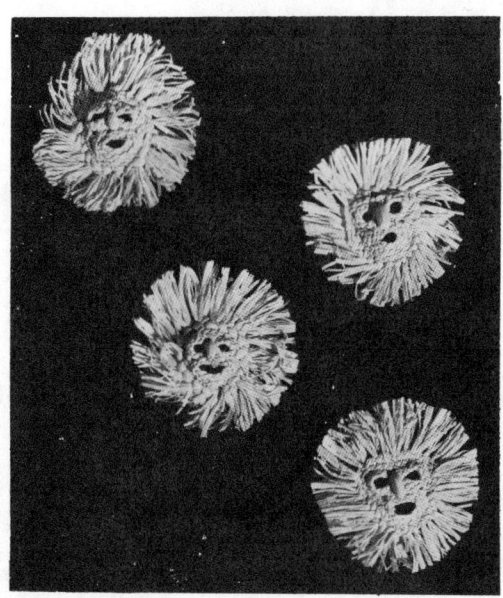

CORN HUSK MASKETTES
Such small images have concealed assets and are used as personal talismans or in dream guessing. These pieces appear not to be consecrated since if they were, four would not be together.
797. No history. Donated by Mrs. Clifford Kirkpatrick. Diameter of masks 2½ inches.

religion as organized about 1800 by the revealer, already mentioned, named Handsome Lake. The term "pagan," which Christians in Canada and the United States have applied to the conservative-minded Iroquois of the Long House religious sect, is disagreeable to the Indians themselves, who have found another term, "deists," to apply to themselves. Nevertheless, the Indian Long House fundamentalists have not been able to shake off the accusation that they are idolators in the esteem of their white countrymen.

Contrary to their popular reputation, however, the Iroquois non-Christians are not adherents of an idolatrous creed. They worship—the word is used with explicit meaning—the Creator, not images, icons, or idols. Their mask images are what the definition in the beginning of this chapter implies; in short, they are dynamic spiritual forces in portraiture, entities animated by the supernatural beings they portray. We must if possible find another term than "idolatry" to satisfy those who insist upon having a learned technical term to describe basic ideas. We on our part may insist that the term chosen should define the idea without adding to or taking away from its meaning. For the Iroquois and other eastern tribes who fashion face images to attract the aid of supernatural beings, as they believe, do not openly or covertly worship such manufactured countenances, and hence "idolatry" is not the name to apply to their rituals. However, since the images are believed to possess latent power to help mankind when respectfully used—a power carried over from an invisible world of mythical creatures who dwell in the deep forests, under water, in the air above or the ground below, and in the darkness—the term "iconism" may be considered appropriate to describe the underlying doctrine. The term at least has the merit of not being overburdened with the old fundamental religious dogma that idolaters are those who "worship false gods," as most Christians have been brought up to believe.

Fenton (1940) summarizes as follows the thought of most ethnologists who have been impressed with the phenomenon of mask images as icons of spirit forces among historic Iroquois and Cherokee and some vicinal Algonkian bands from the St. Lawrence to the Carolinas: "Finally, to place the complex of Iroquois masked shamanism in ethnographic perspective the comparative method might be employed. If we can show that the complex has a historical depth reaching back to the first white contacts with the Iroquois, it would be relevant to investigate whether the Iroquois possess the complex in a greater degree than their Algonquian neighbors. If we could determine the center whence masking spread throughout the northeast, some light might shine on the problem of whether Iroquois masking is a diagnostic trait pointing to their alleged southern origin, or whether it is related to northern shamanism and the use

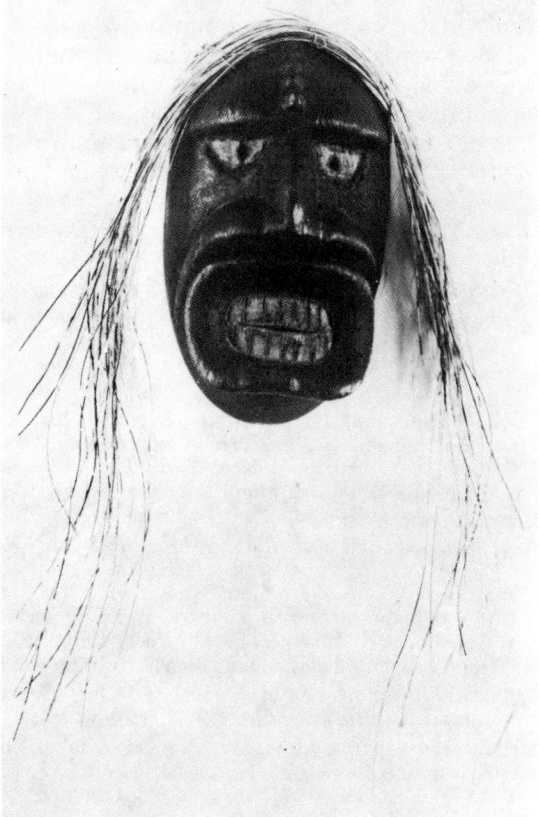

ONONDAGA
MASKETTE

Such miniature masks are used in curing rites when the chiefs have guessed the cause of a patient's sickness. The maskette is given to the healed patient as a charm to protect against return of the ailment. This wooden mask has its face painted red. Some others are black.

3193. Six Nations Reserve. F. G. Speck, who obtained this from Nicodemus Peters, a Delaware-Munsee, who had it from an Onondaga. Height 2 inches.

of masks across the Arctic littoral, or whether the complex was original with the Iroquois themselves from whom it spread to the neighboring Delaware."

To these observations the author is tempted to add some comments, not necessarily conclusive in thought, arising out of material derived from Delaware sources specifically and eastern Algonkian in general, and relating to the rise and spread of masking customs in the east.

Starting with the historical axiom that no group of people, large or small, dwells in isolation, we may look for the effects of the give and take principle on the building of cultures. The Iroquois have been givers on a large scale, and they have likewise been takers.

To the Algonkian tribes surrounding them they have passed on so much that we have little idea of its extent as yet. Primarily the whole maize culture of the northeast is attributable to their importation of material and methods of horticulture. Advanced techniques in weaving, splint basketry for example, may have come northeast through similar channels. However, it is chiefly in respect to social, political, and religious organization that ideas emanating from the south-central regions of the continent had crept over the horizon to enter the cultures of the Algonkian area of the northeastern woodlands. This puts us in touch with the problem of masks in the ritual and myth of eastern tribes.

The following tribes east of the Mississippi are known to have used masks in religious or dramatic performances.

Eastern Tribes Using Masks

Iroquoian tribes of the northern area. The Huron and extinguished nations affiliated with them, formerly occupying southern Ontario and the eastern Great Lakes portions of New York. The Five Nations of central, northern, and western New York, comprising the Mohawk, Oneida, Onondaga, Cayuga, and Seneca, still resident in the area.

Algonkian tribes of the Atlantic slope. The Lenape subdivisions, the Munsee and Mahican, constituting the Delaware Nation of historic times, resident in the Hudson Valley, southern New York, New Jersey, and eastern Pennsylvania until the nineteenth century, and now surviving in Oklahoma, Kansas, Wisconsin, and Ontario. The Shawnee, formerly dispersed over parts of the Carolinas, Pennsylvania, and the central states, and now in Oklahoma.

Iroquoian tribes of the near southeast. The Cherokee in the Great Smoky Mountains of North Carolina, still residing there.

Siouan tribes of the southeast. The Catawba of South Carolina, who in the early eighteenth century performed a mask ceremony described by Lawson (1714). The Tutelo of western Virginia and North Carolina, who traditionally used masks.

Thus the distribution of face images appears to be uneven over the eastern region. Intervening between the tribes that used them were the Powhatan group of Virginia (Algonkian) and the Nanticoke affiliates of Maryland and Delaware, concerning whom no references to masks are to be found in the records or traditions. North and east of the Iroquois and Mahican the sources are silent on the same point. Within historic times the Muskhogian nations of the southeast, constituting the Creek Confederation, have not been noted as users of masks. Nothing exists to show that the Chippewa, the Algonquin proper, or the Central Algonkian ever employed them. However, the archaeological evidence along these lines is affirmative, showing that masks of wood were known to the ancient inhabitants of the southern Florida Gulf coast before the Seminole (Muskhogian) settled there. In Tennessee and western Virginia

74

conch shell face images have been excavated in sufficient number to prove their use among the prehistoric populations still unfortunately unclassified as to language and tribal identity.

An answer to the question of the origin of masked shamanism, as raised by Fenton, still remains beyond our grasp, but several suggestions present themselves upon consideration of the circumstances so far revealed.

The Iroquois and Huron have presumably been the agents of diffusion of face images among the Delawares, Munsee and Mahican, as far east as the Hudson Valley, and probably among the Shawnee of the Ohio Valley. The use of masks across the eastern, northern, and western boundaries of Iroquois influence by contact ceases abruptly in historic times, but the boundary on the south and southwest is open through the findings of archaeology. Students of Iroquoian prehistory are looking in this quarter, the drainage system of the Ohio and Cumberland and Tennessee, for the junction locality where the back tracks of the Iroquois and Cherokee converge, to account for their structurally related languages. Both Iroquois and Cherokee have carried down certain phases of an ancient mask

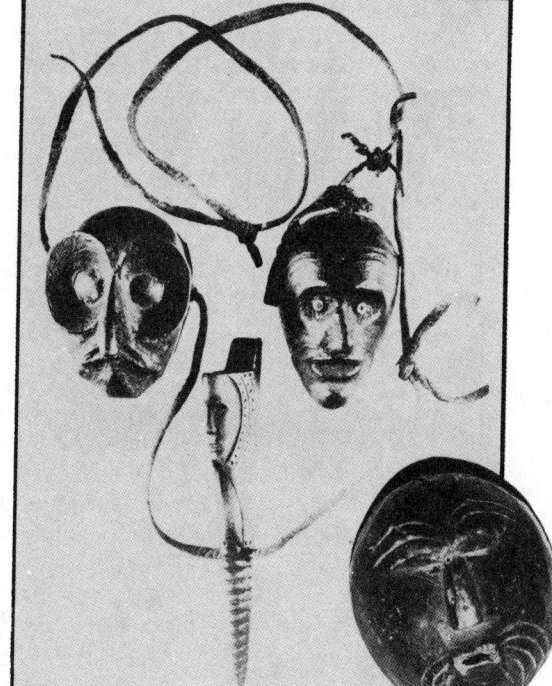

MINIATURE MASK

Photographed against the background of similar specimens supposedly from the Delaware, this maskette may be from that Alnonkian tribe too though it was obtained from Andrew Sprague, a Tuscarora. The Iroquois use similar faces in the curing of disease.

1625. Caledonia, Ontario, 1922. M. G. Chandler.

75

tradition and types of dancing, dance music, and musical instruments, and the southern mountaineer Cherokee can be proposed as disseminators of the mask complex in the southern Appalachians as the Iroquois can for the northern area. The lapse of time, say five hundred years, separating the northern and southern branches of the Iroquoian stock from their common parentage of speech, could account for the wide differences noted between mask shamanism in the rituals of Iroquois medicine societies and the masked dramatic performances of the Cherokee.

However, it should not be overlooked that over the entire middle Atlantic Coast region stationary wooden face images of spiritual beings stood in and about the open places or buildings where religious ceremonies and sepulchral rites took place. From Pamlico Sound on the seaboard of Carolina, through the Powhatan area of Tidewater Virginia, to the Delawares and Munsee of New York and Pennsylvania, the carved and painted image posts bearing likenesses of greater and lesser deities are known, through accounts of early explorers and among some of the surviving groups of the original tribes, to be properties of Algonkian religious culture.

However, face images in the form of portable masks and face images carved on stationary posts are different things. They represent different classes of mythical beings among the peoples from whom we have factual data, and their functions in religion are different. The Iroquois and Cherokee have only the portable masks, so far as is known; the Delawares and related peoples have both forms of images; while the southern coastal Powhatan and Carolina Algonkians had only the face images carved on posts.

In concluding this brief analysis of masking phenomena among the Iroquois and their neighbor groups a conjectural answer to the questions raised may be risked. From facts already known concerning Iroquois and Cherokee masked performances,* spiced with a dash of intuitive imagination, it seems probable that in early times the tribes from the Hudson to the Carolina Sound area, in the central sector of eastern Algonkian occupation, knew and practised certain rites connected with graven face images on posts; that the early Iroquoian peoples performed rites with face mask images in various usages distinct from those of the Algonkian; and that the Delawares and Munsee adjacent to and culturally influenced by the Iroquois adopted the use of mask images from them, in addition to their own stationary icons, and developed the functions of both.

---

*The author refers to several monographic studies, dealing with Cayuga Iroquois and Cherokee ceremonies and dances, which he has completed but which are as yet unpublished.

While masks play a most important rôle in the religious life of the Iroquois, there are other appurtenances required in ceremonial performance which claim the attention of those viewing museum exhibits.

Of primary importance are rhythm-producing instruments which accent the melodies of the dance rituals and "prop up the songs," as the Indians say. They are correctly called musical instruments if it is understood that in this instance the term denotes tympanic instruments that produce but one tone pitch. The orchestral list includes drum, hand rattles, striking sticks, and, in one Cayuga dance game, the notched rasp. The drum and the rattles of different types are held in semisacred esteem.

Every material used in their construction is symbolical of some phylum or class of animal and plant life that contributes its sub-

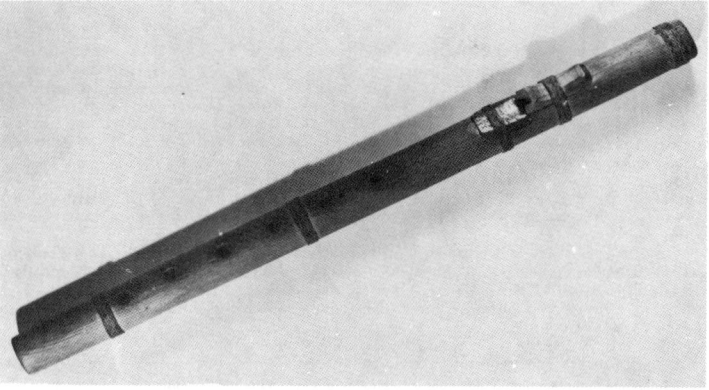

COURTING FLUTE

The flute was the only native wind instrument. It was not used in any ceremony but was devoted solely to musical relaxation.

2113. Six Nations Reserve, 1916-18. M. G. Chandler.

stance to the life support of the people. It is not easy for modern folk to sense the feeling of communion of spirit that underlies the use of a turtle's shell, splints of hickory, threads of animal sinew, animal skin wrappings, and kernels of maize, combined in the making of a large snapping turtle shell rattle and blended into the purpose of the man who uses such a combination of spirit forces as a rhythm marker to accompany his voice. But to the native believer in the faith of his Iroquois ancestors it is easy and obvious. With another kind of rattle, formed of the whole rind of a gourd or a squash, he sings the chants that express his dependence upon and thanks to the forces beyond him for the blessings of the fruits of

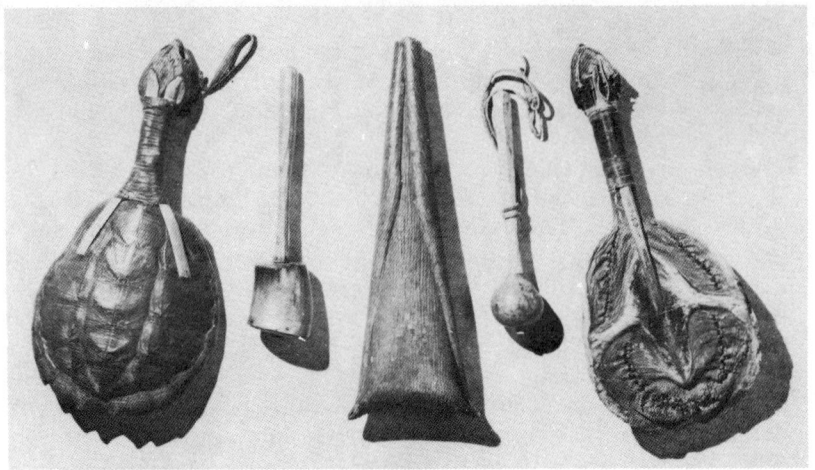

RATTLES

"In Iroquoian cosmology the very earth rests on the back of a snapping turtle, and rattles made from its whole carapace and plastron with the head and neck stretched over a stick inserted to form the handle were described by seventeenth-century explorers who observed the Iroquois. Turtle rattles are still being made and singers consistently employ them to beat out the tempo for the two dances that are characteristically Iroquois—Great Feather Dance and the Dance of the False-faces with whom the turtle rattle is standard equipment. A turtle rattle about 10 inches to a foot long, including the handle is considered best for singing. The singer sits astride a wooden bench and beats out the measures between his knees, striking the board on which he sits with the edge of the turtle shell. It takes a good singer to raise his voice above the din.

"Gourds are still raised among the Six Nations for containers and especially to make rattles for 'pumpkin shakes,' as meetings of the Medicine Men's fraternity are colloquially called. A summer squash will do almost as well." (Fenton.)

Horn rattles may originally have been made of bison horn but are now almost invariably of cow horn.

Hickory bark rattles were made by doubling over a piece of bark so that one half partly embraces the other and so seals it except for the end which is plugged. Beauchamp (1905) wrote of this type of rattle that it was then old and quite rare.

1613. New York State. Milwaukee Public Museum. 2120. Six Nations Reserve, 1916-18. 1623. New York State. 2119. Six Nations Reserve, 1916-18. 2111. New York State Seneca, 1916-18. All but first, M. G. Chandler.

agriculture. Symbolism lurks in almost every material object utilized and every action performed in the course of Iroquois ceremonies. The Long House itself, in which the rites are enacted, is a symbol of the universe of the Iroquois. The formal movements of the dance periods and the bodily motions of the dancers are also implicit symbols.

These are only a few examples of the kind of nature appreciation so deeply set in the Indian mind and so feebly felt by most persons reared in European culture environments. In short, the unchristianized Iroquois lives, much as his forerunners did, in a realm of symbols, operating and expressing himself by them. To those who have minds receptive to the wider horizons of thought concerning spirits

RATTLES

Left: A Cayuga tortoise shell rattle formerly used in the Woman's Dance. Though the rattle is from Sour Springs longhouse, the tortoise is not known to occur near this reserve and this type of rattle has been so long out of use in Cayuga rites that the specimen was probably brought with the tribe from New York State. (Speck.)

Center: Painted gourd rattle used by the Medicine or Big Rattle Society. The black and red decorations were said by its user to symbolize "night," the time of the Society's meetings. (Speck.)

Right: Seneca rattle made of a warty gourd, used in rituals connected with vegetation.

3189. Six Nations Reserve, 1932. F. G. Speck. 3188. As above. 3187. Allegheny Reserve, New York. F. G. Speck.

and the creations of nature the museum collections demonstrate these attitudes of the Iroquois.

No less than sixteen variant forms of sound-producing instruments have been noted by the author among the Cayuga in Canada, representing perhaps the high mark of Iroquois musical evolution. Of this number eleven are employed to strike the measure for the dance songs. As for the dance songs, it would be no exaggeration to say that almost five hundred, in a dozen chant series, have been heard in a single night of ceremonial festivity lasting about ten hours, that is, between past sunset and near dawn. The musicians—singers, drummers, and rattle shakers—are all men.

In respect to the quality of Iroquois music in the esteem of one who was not brought up in its tradition, the author must acknowledge that he has never heard more beautiful melodies or sweeter sounding male voices in unison than those he has listened to in the Long House. The talents of no trained musicologist, not even those of George Herzog himself, can adequately transcribe the intangible qualities they possess or convey by a modern system of notation an adequate notion of the emotional effect of the melodies chanted through the winter night by a chorus of Iroquois singers.

The Iroquois have never invented a stringed instrument. Indeed, the believers of the native creed have been taught by their revealer, Handsome Lake, that the violin is a cursed instrument, and even to listen to it is considered a sin. The only native wind instrument is a flageolet having six finger stops and blown at the end. It is not used

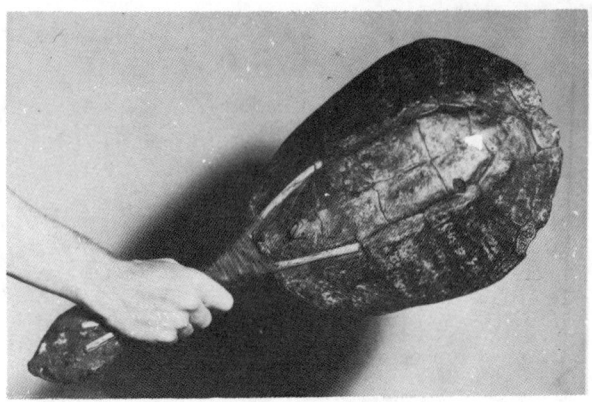

LARGE TURTLE RATTLE

This specimen from the Cayuga is of a large snapping turtle. This form of big rattle (*Kaniate Stawedra*) is used only in wooden False Face Society rituals, with the masks, and also in the Great Feather Dance on the fourth and fifth days of the Midwinter, or New Year Ceremony at Sour Springs Longhouse. Length 23½ inches.

3752. From Sadeganhes (of the Turtle Clan). Six Nations Reserve. F. G. Speck.

in any ceremony but is devoted solely to pleasurable musical relaxation. Some ethnologists consider it to be an acquisition from Europeans. The conch shell horn, which fifty years ago the Cayuga sounded to call the worshippers to the Long House, is thought by some Indians to have come from a similar source.

The Iroquois water drum is an object of distinction, both in function and in musical quality. Only one type of drum is used throughout the series of dance rites, which total over twenty among Seneca, Cayuga, Onondaga, and Oneida communicants of the Long House religion. Most of the dance rituals call for use of the drum. In comparison with those of other tribes of the east the Iroquois water drum is small. It is seldom more than five or six inches in diameter. The body is made of sections of wood fitted tightly together in the fashion of a pail, with a disc bottom, a stretched skin head covers the top, which has a diameter a little less than that of the bottom, and the whole is held taut by a snug hoop. The drum is made watertight, for it is essential that the tone be soft and vibrant from a small amount of water held in the drum. A tap stick, not a beater, is bounced upon the skin head to produce the musical tone required as an accompaniment to the voices of the ritual singers. The stick is balanced between the fingers of the drummer and used lightly. The drum head, which is kept moist, gives a vibration that possesses definite tone. Drummers are extremely particular in tuning the drum to a certain pitch before the chanting is begun. To the Indians the drum and all its parts are more than mere objects of manufacture.

They are themselves spiritual entities and are treated with due respect. The drumstick shown among the illustrations is one of the most elaborately carved examples, almost a treasure of Iroquois art in wood.

Rattles are an essential part of Iroquois music making. With few exceptions the dance song-rituals are punctuated with the ringing rhythm of rattles in the hands of the singers. Like the drum, these rattles are objects of respect. The rattle in most general use during the last century is one made of a section of cow horn scraped down thin and pierced with a wooden handle. Among the different tribes of the Iroquois group the rattles are fairly uniform, both in shape and in plainness of style. Tradition tells that before the coming of the whites and the introduction of cattle these Indians made rattles of elm bark, and some of the Cayuga traditionalists can still produce them. The rattling accompaniment to dances is furnished by two to ten singers, each with his horn rattle. These singers form the orchestra, which sits on a long bench in the mid-space of the dance floor in the Long House.

In the ritual of several important dances, such as the false face society dance (in which wooden mask images are worn) and the Great Feather Dance performed in obedience to the will of the Creator, the soft swishing of the horn rattles gives way to an almost thunderous hammering of the huge turtle shell rattles. The instrument is constructed of the entire shell of the snapping turtle, *Chelydra serpentina,* including the head and neck, after the legs, tail, and internals have been removed. The extended neck skin, with the head dried in place at its end, is held in place with splints. The rattlers inside the shell are usually dried corn kernels. Each member of the false face society of shaman doctors properly owns and carries one of these instruments in his performance. For their dance the orchestra consists of two singers, who straddle the bench in the middle of the floor space, beating upon it with similar rattles. The great snapping turtle shell rattle is a distinctive instrument of the Iroquois and is employed by no other people in America except the Delaware and Munsee, among whom it is used only in the pantomime of the masked dancer, who wears a painted wooden face image. The use of rattle and mask together confirms the supposition of an Iroquois derivation.

BISON HORN RATTLE
3002. Cattaraugus Reservation, New York. Albert G. Heath.

Other types of rattles are known to the Iroquois and are generally associated with specific dance rituals. Among those illustrated are the one-piece folded hickory bark instrument, more common among the Seneca, and the gourd rattle, sometimes formed of an entire gourd, sometimes of a gourd with the neck cut off and a wooden handle substituted. It is used in rites connected with the growing of crops. The hand instrument, often lacking a handle, of the female singer who leads the Woman's Dance chant, is made from the shell of a small turtle—the snapping turtle, painted turtle (*Chrysemys picta*), or, anciently, a box turtle (*Terrapene carolina*).

FOOD BOWLS AND PADDLE

Wooden bowls were used in the preparation of food, in the game of dice, for drinking and medicine. These bowls are unusually large. The short paddle is of the type used by both Iroquois and Delaware for lifting corn bread.

Upper bowl: 2241. The reservation near Lake Cayuga, N. Y. Length 25 inches. *Lower bowl*: 1626. Oneida. Near Appleton, Wisconsin. Length 26 inches. *Food Paddle*: 2110. Six Nations Reserve, 1916-18. Length 16½ inches. All M. G. Chandler.

BOWLS, SPOONS, AND LADLES

Among other noteworthy objects in the ceremonial equipment of the Iroquois are wooden bowls, spoons, huge ladles, and pot stirrers. Those utensils regularly used in the Long House by the individuals and committees who manage the programs have a semisacred status.

The large bowl, made of a maple or elm burl in former times but replaced nowadays by a lathe-turned bowl, plays a prominent part in the rite performed on the last day of the five- to seven-day festival known as the Annual Winter or New Year ceremony. The rite is called the Bowl Game; yet it is not merely a game but rather a sacred wagering ritual, considered to have been introduced to mankind by the Creator as a sanctified amusement to bring joy and relaxation following the seriousness of the period of devotion. Each Long House group of worshippers preserves a bowl of this kind, along with six dice of dried peach pits and the beans used for

BELT CUP

Though the provinence of this cup is unknown it is illustrated here on the basis that the Iroquois are known to have used round-bottomed wooden cups for drinking. Speck observes: "The cup figured is to all appearances one of the drinking cups made and used by Indians of the east and north, and like many of the Indian wares extensively taken over by trade or exchange by white settlers in the opening of the century. I have collected similar forms from modern Indian groups as follows: Abenaki, Iroquois, Tuscarora, Penobscot, Montagnais, Huron as I well remember, and have seen them from other regions in eastern Canada and New England. Among the northern tribes they were carried by a thong attached to a belt with a slip-toggle. It is said that women took them along to drink from when going berry-picking. Northern Indians do not drink by putting the mouth to the water like dogs, etc. One other reason is that disease (evil spirit forms) lurk in the water and might be swallowed. Like the wooden spoons, bowls, stirrers, etc., these cups were given to whites or traded to them for their beauty and appeal as well as use. This one of yours, I should say, is from one of the eastern Algonkian or central Algonkian tribes (maybe Ojibwa, Potawatomi, Menomini, or Ottawa) and is a rare piece. The curved handle carried is decidedly like the crookneck handle on spoons, therefore strictly Indian in type." Ours may be copied from the ceramic cups of the whites, but worn on the belt.

The cup, made of a burl, is beautifully smooth and worn thin on edges and bottom, thus giving evidence of long use. When received it bore an old label reading: "This Indian drinking cup known to have been in the Vaningen family since 1776. Mrs. Levi Vaningen, Plymouth, Michigan." Inquiry at Plymouth in 1942 failed to locate any family of that name.

Dr. Arthur C. Parker, in personal communication, observes that the cup is much like one he received from the Scaticooks (Mohicans, Algonkian stock) of the Hudson River, being perhaps the last relic of the groups that lived at Pine Plains, Dutchess County, New York. Another similar cup made by a Scaticook Indian in the mid-eighteenth century is in the Museum of the American Indian. It is figured by Heye in *Indian Notes and Monographs*, Vol. 5, No. 2, 1921.

1160. Detroit, 1942. R. T. Hatt.

counters of the score earned by each side. In Seneca thought the Bowl Game, or wager as Fenton calls it, "symbolizes the struggle of the good brother, the Creator, with his evil twin brother for the control of the earth."

The carved spoons, generally of maple wood or, like the bowls, made of burls, are the personal cherished property of individuals,

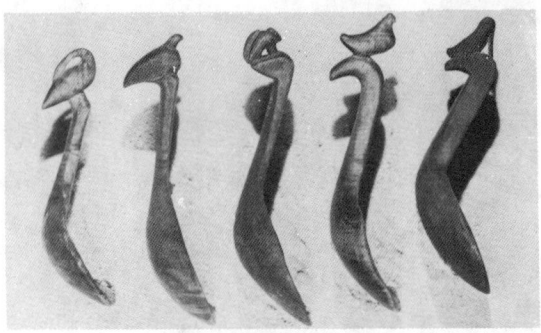

ONEIDA WOODEN SPOONS

Carved spoons are the cherished property of individuals and are brought to the festivals for use in eating foods in the longhouse as a sacrament. From left to right the effigies may be identified as swan, grouse, squirrel, grouse, and woodcock.

2124, 2242, 2123, 2126, 2125. Oneida Reserve, Wisconsin, 1916-1926. M. G. Chandler.

who bring them to festivals to use in eating the ceremonial foods consumed in the Long House as a sacrament. Effigy carving on the handle of a spoon occasionally depicts the clan animal or "totem" of its owner. The carvings rate highly as examples of good taste in art.

Ladles and stirrers of maple or hickory for the feasting caldrons from which the meats and corn foods are portioned to the devout are also part of the Long House furniture. Their beauty lies not in carved figures but in the polished grain of the wood, brought out by years of immersion in grease, and in their grace of form.

WAMPUM

Other objects sought by museums as examples of the gentler aspects of Iroquois life are strings and strips of wampum. The sacredness of the shell material, made into cylindrical beads averaging less than a quarter inch in length and about an eighth of an inch in diameter drilled through the long axis, has long been known as a characteristic of the culture of the Iroquois and the eastern Algonkian tribes. Wampum is a symbol of steadfastness of word pledged in civil and political agreements, in contracts of marriage, and in other binding ties between individuals or groups, and of sincerity of heart with respect to motives and statements and in devotional actions. Its most noteworthy historical function, however, has been that of a means of recording and preserving the articles of treaty negotiations between nations and party groups entering into relations. For such use large bands called "belts," the width of a hand and from several feet to several yards long, were woven of white and dark-blue wampum beads arranged to form simple designs. The belts were constructed in duplicate, and one was kept by each of the contracting parties as a memorial of the event. Wampum belts could not be read literally, but were interpretable by those who had memorized the design symbols. They were held in veneration by the eastern Indians with a depth of sentiment difficult for the European to understand.

With all the references to wampum and its functions in historical literature handed down to us by scribes for over two centuries, there is much still to be learned about it. Wampum was and is used by the Iroquois in connection with ceremonies, but its chief use is as a medium of conveying messages and summonses. At the time of the New Year Ceremony it is "touched" by the penitent as a pledge of heart in a rite of confession of sins and canceling of grievances.

SACRED PLANTS

Tobacco is a sacred plant esteemed by the Iroquois as one of the blessings bestowed upon them by the Creator. Smoking and burning it in the fire as a "sacrifice offering" is another form of pledging sincerity of mind and heart. There is scarcely a rite performed by individuals or by medicine society groups but has its interval for the burning of tobacco. The tobacco employed is not the commercial product but the native-grown leaves, taken from plants raised from seed handed down from the far-off past.

The ancient and native food staples, regarded as gifts from the Creator, are also held in holy esteem. The original products of the vital harvest comprise maize, beans, and squash, the juice of forest berries, and maple sap. There is also the flesh of animals destined to be eaten by man. Strange, from our point of view, is the discovery that fish are relatively unimportant both in the diet of the Iroquois and in the amount of attention given them as food blessings in the rituals of the Iroquois ceremonial cycle. It would seem that this observation may have a bearing upon the location of an earlier habitat of the Iroquois, and perhaps is ecologically significant in relation to their migration.

For a very long period Iroquois culturation has progressed along lines of horticultural experimentation. Iroquois successes in this field include discovery of the curative values of herbs and the ingredients of remedies derived from other natural resources in a broad domain. In most of their religious festivals the gift-blessings of food are partaken of in thankful spirit and expressed in prayer and dance rituals. To the Iroquois foods and medicines are much the same in action and result—health and nutrition combined in the normal life they strive to lead. Out of this rationalized background come the working principles of their religious philosophy. In the

85

symbolical ceremonies they celebrate, the two life-maintaining principles are appealed to in song and dance movement invoking the food givers and the health restorers and protectors who, as lesser deities, carry out the plans of the Creator.

MEDICINE SOCIETIES

Numerous medicine societies flourish in the native religious system. Fenton lists eleven among the Seneca and Onondaga of New York. The author has noted a total of nineteen among the Cayuga across the international border, though this relatively high number includes companies having both restricted and unrestricted membership and so the list is not strictly comparable to Fenton's.

Since the medicine societies mark the high point of the organization principle for which Iroquois culture has ever been noted, they are listed below.

MEDICINE SOCIETIES OF THE IROQUOIS

SENECA AND ONONDAGA (NEW YORK)*	CAYUGA (ONTARIO)†	
	Restricted	*Unrestricted*
Bear	Bear	Snow-snake Rite
Buffalo	White Buffalo	Chipmunk Rite
Eagle	Eagle	Thunder Rite and
False-face	Wooden False-face	Lacrosse Rite
Husk-face	Corn-husk Mask	War (Wasáse) Dance
Little Water	Dark Dance	Chicken Dance
Mystic Animals	Medicine Man's	Striking-stick Dance
Otter, or Dark Dance	Otter	Ghost Dance Rite
Charm Holders		Dream-guessing Rite
Changing Ribs		Dreamer, or Fortune
Chanters of the Dead		Teller, Rite
		Tug-of-war, or
*From Fenton (1936).		Pulling, Rite
†From the author's manuscripts.		Football Rite

The restricted medicine societies limit their membership, and their major curing rites are conducted in private sessions in the homes of the sick. Yet they can scarcely be called secret societies, as some have thought they were. In the unrestricted societies participation is open to persons who may wish to further the curing process by joining with the performers, thus augmenting the force of appeal to the societies' tutelaries through strength of numbers and concentration of wish for the recovery of the patient.

The members and associates of these bodies of doctor shamans also enact their rites publicly in the Long House, as a part of the same series of programs with the general worship ceremonies. That the two orders of service belong together in the festivals of a religion of health is obvious to the Iroquois.

The modern form of worship of the Iroquois, as carried out in five Long House congregations in Canada and four in New York, shows indications of religious acculturation brought about, as Fenton has determined, through the influence of Quaker missionaries. The Seneca prophet and revealer Handsome Lake, who founded the creed now followed by those of the ancient faith, imbibed teachings from a mission of the Society of Friends established at Cold Spring near the close of the eighteenth century. It was then that Handsome Lake experienced his trance visions and translation to the spirit world.

The moral aspects of religion, embodied in a so-called code, were taught the Iroquois by Handsome Lake. The code was discussed and in large part published by Parker(1912B). The injunctions and sermonettes of the code, which comprises over a hundred commandments, are memorized by self-appointed leaders and are recited periodically when the faithful convene for ceremonies in the Long House. Their moral sageness, simplicity, and soundness, even under the scrutiny of skeptics, amply justify the name they bear in the Iroquois tongues—*Gaiwiiye*, the Good Word.

One general observation remains to be added to this sketch of the religious content of Iroquois culture, considered as that of a group of closely related tribes. Recent students of Iroquois institutions realize that before the formation of the League of the Iroquois, let us say quickly about five hundred years ago, these tribes were independent unit groups. Traditions of Deganawidah, conceiver and founder of the league, point to the existence of an unharmonious state of intertribal affairs at the time the league was founded. With the establishment of peace between the tribes came a period of closer social contact. It follows that conditions then tended toward the leveling of differences in their organized life and economy. However, the differentiated beginnings of the tribes, minor as the variations may have been, would account for such differences as are revealed through investigation of the same tribes in later times. Intensive study in the widely separated settlements of the Iroquois of today shows that while the universal pattern of Iroquois social and religious organization prevails among them all, the details vary. Before an adequate synthesis of Iroquois culturation can be made the various groups must be approached independently and interviewed in the round. A dozen such groups and bands of the Iroquois await attention in locations extending from New York to Ontario and Quebec, and even to Wisconsin and Oklahoma.

Here we may leave the story of Iroquois religion, its abstract notions and its peace and health insuring aspects briefly outlined, to be told by the exhibits. The series of objects upon which we depend for exposition of so subjective a topic come largely from still existent groups of those Indians who style themselves "Keepers of the Faith," and whose tenacity of creed is comparable to that of Christians who sing "Faith of our fathers, holy faith, we will be true to thee till death."

Archaeology reveals the antiquity of some of the objects still used in native rites. The full story remains, a living epic in the minds and religious behavior of some two thousand Iroquois who maintain the creed of the Long House. Year after year its ceremonies revolve in their orderly cycle, the charm of the soft sweet music and the teachings of coöperation and love of mankind exerting their appeal upon a growing audience of the Iroquois people, who turn to the native way of worship for solace in times of stress.

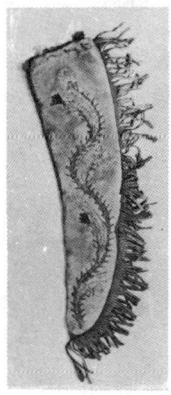

HURON KNIFE SHEATH

The sheath is of commercially tanned leather, (probably India elk), decorated with moosehair embroidery.

2134. Niagara Falls, N. Y., 1928. M. G. Chandler.

References Cited and Consulted

The following list includes publications cited in the text and those from which material has been drawn. Unless otherwise stated the author is responsible for other data, which are taken from his unpublished manuscripts and field notes. The voluminous early historical sources dealing with peoples of the Iroquoian area have not been included by title in the list. For a full bibliography of matter pertaining to the ethnology of the Iroquoian tribes (Conestoga, Erie, Huron, Iroquois, Neutral, Cherokee, Tuscarora, Meherrin, Nottoway), the reader is referred to G. P. Murdock, *Ethnographic Bibliography of North America*, Yale Anthropological Series, Volume 1, New Haven, 1941.

BARBEAU, C. M.

1915. Huron and Wyandot Mythology. Ottawa: Memoirs of the Canadian Department of Mines, Geological Survey, Vol. XLVI.

1917. Iroquoian clans and phratries. American Anthropologist, n.s., Vol. XIX, No. 4.

1928. The origin of floral and other designs among the Canadian and neighboring Indians. Proceedings, 33d International Congress of Americanists, New York.

n.d. (about 1928). Assomption Sash. Ottawa: National Museum of Canada, Bulletin 93, Anthropological Series, No. 24.

1940. Indian Trade Silver. Ottawa: Transactions of the Royal Society, Section II.

BEAUCHAMP, W. M.

1902. Horn and Bone Implements of the New York Indians. Albany: New York State Museum Bulletin L.

1903. Metallic Ornaments of the New York Indians. Albany: New York State Museum Bulletin LXXIII.

1905. Aboriginal Use of Wood in New York. Albany: New York State Museum Bulletin LXXXIX.

BESTON, HENRY

1942. The St. Lawrence. New York: Farrar & Rinehart.

BLOOM, LEONARD

1942. The acculturation of the eastern Cherokee. North Carolina Historical Review, Vol. XIX, No. 4.

BRINTON, D. G.

1891. The American Race. New York.

BUSHNELL, D. I., Jr.

1934. Tribal Migrations East of the Mississippi. Washington: Smithsonian Miscellaneous Collections, Vol. 89, No. 12.

CHAMBERLAIN, A. F.
   1904. Iroquois in northwestern Canada. American Anthropologist, Vol. 6, No. 4.

COLDEN, CADWALLADER
   1922. History of the Five Nations of Canada. New York, 2 vols. (Originally published in London, 1755.)

CONVERSE, H. M.
   1902. The Iroquois Silver Brooches. Albany: Fifty-ninth Report of the New York State Museum, 1900.

DOUGLAS, F. H.
   1931. Iroquois Foods. Denver Art Museum, Department of Indian Art, Leaflet 26.
   1934. (2d, 1937.) Design Areas in Indian Art. Denver Art Museum, Department of Indian Art, Leaflet 62.

DOUGLAS, F. H. and RENE D'HARNONCOURT
   1941. Indian Art of the United States. New York: Museum of Modern Art.

FENTON, W. N.
   1936. A. An Outline of Seneca Ceremonies at Cold Spring Longhouse. New Haven: Yale University Publications in Anthropology, No. 9.
          B. A Further Quest for Iroquois Medicines. Washington: Explorations and Field Work of the Smithsonian Institution.
   1937. The Seneca society of faces. Scientific Monthly, Vol. XLIV.
   1940. A. Problems Arising from the Historic Northeastern Position of the Iroquois. Washington: Smithsonian Miscellaneous Collections, Vol. 100.
          B. An Herbarium from the Allegany Senecas. Historical Annals of Southwestern New York. New York: Lewis Historical Publishing Company.
          C. Museum and Field Studies of Iroquois Masks and Ritualism. Washington: Explorations and Field Work of the Smithsonian Institution in 1940.
   1941. A. Tonawanda Longhouse Ceremonies Ninety Years after Lewis Henry Morgan. Washington: Smithsonian Institution, Anthropological Papers, No. 15, Bulletin 128.
          B. Masked Medicine Societies of the Iroquois. Washington: Smithsonian Institution, Report 1940.
   1942. Songs from the Iroquois Longhouse. Washington: Smithsonian Institution, Publication 3691.

GILBERT, W. H.
   1943. The Eastern Cherokees. Washington: Smithsonian Institution, Anthropological Papers, No. 23.

GILLINGHAM, H. E.
   1934. Indián silver ornaments. Pennsylvania Magazine of History and Biography, Vol. LXVII, No. 2.
   1937. Indian Silver Ornaments Made by Philadelphia Silversmiths. New York: Museum of the American Indian, Heye Foundation.

GILLINGHAM, H. E.—*continued*

1943. Indian trade and silver ornaments made by Joseph Richardson, Jr. Pennsylvania Magazine of History and Biography, Vol. LXVII, No. 1.

GOLDENWEISER, A. A.

1912. Report on Iroquois Work. Reports from the Anthropological Division, Sessional Paper No. 26, Ottawa.

1913. Geological Survey of Canada. Reports from the Anthropological Division, Sessional Paper No. 26.

1922. Early Civilization. New York: Alfred A. Knopf.

1937. Anthropology: An Introduction to Primitive Culture. New York: F. S. Crofts.

GRIFFIN, J. B.

1943. The Fort Ancient Aspect: Its Cultural and Chronological Position in Mississippi Valley Archaeology. Ann Arbor: University of Michigan Press.

1944. The Iroquois in American Prehistory. Ann Arbor: Papers of the Michigan Academy of Science, Arts, and Letters, Vol. XXIX.

HARRINGTON, M. R.

1908. A. Iroquois Silverwork. New York: American Museum of Natural History, Anthropological Papers, Vol. 1, Part VI.
B. Some Seneca corn-foods and their preparation. American Anthropologist, n.s., Vol. 10, No. 4.

HEWITT, J. N. B.

1907–10. Articles on Iroquois tribes (Onondaga, Mohawk, Seneca, Oneida, Cayuga) in Handbook of the American Indian. Washington: Bureau of American Ethnology, Bulletin 30.

1916. A Constitutional League of Peace in the Stone Age of North America. Washington: Annual Report of the Smithsonian Institution.

1918. Exploration and Field Work of the Smithsonian Institution. Washington: Smithsonian Miscellaneous Collections, Vol. 66, No. 17.

1933. Fiftieth Annual Report of the Bureau of American Ethnology, 1932–33. Washington: Smithsonian Institution.

HUNT, G. T.

1940. The Wars of the Iroquois: A Study in Intertribal Trade Relations. Madison: University of Wisconsin Press.

HUNTER, H. V.

1940. The Ethnography of Salt in Aboriginal North America. Dissertation for the degree of Master of Arts, University of Pennsylvania.

JAMIESON, N. E.

1942. Indian Arts and Crafts. Six Nations Indians Yesterday and Today. Ontario: Six Nations Agricultural Society.

JENNESS, DIAMOND

1934. The Indians of Canada. Ottawa: National Museum of Canada, Bulletin 65.

KEPPLER, JOSEPH
  1941. Comments on Certain Iroquois Masks. New York: Museum of the American Indian, Heye Foundation, Vol. XII, No. 4.

KNOWLES, NATHANIEL
  1940. The Torture of Captives by the Indians of Eastern North America. Dissertation for the degree of Doctor of Philosophy, University of Pennsylvania.

KRAUS, B. S.
  1944. Acculturation, a new approach to the Iroquoian problem. American Antiquity, Vol. IX, No. 3.

KROEBER, A. L.
  1939. Cultural and Natural Areas of Native North America. Berkeley: University of California Press.

LISMER, MARJORIE
  1941. Seneca Splint Basketry. Indian Handicraft Pamphlets No. 4. Washington: U. S. Department of the Interior.

MOONEY, JAMES
  1910-11. Articles on Cherokee, Meherrin, Nottoway, in Handbook of the American Indian. Washington: Bureau of American Ethnology, Bulletin 30.
  1928. The Aboriginal Population of America North of Mexico. Washington: Smithsonian Miscellaneous Collections, Vol. 80, No. 7.

MORGAN, L. H.
  1850. Report on the Indian Collections: Fabrics, Inventions and Utensils of the Iroquois. Albany: Annual Report to the Regents of the University of New York, III.
  1851. Report on the Fabrics, Inventions, Implements and Utensils of the Iroquois. Albany: Annual Report to the Regents of the University of New York, V.
  1851. League of the Ho-dé-no-sau-nee, or Iroquois. Rochester: Sage & Brothers. (Reprinted 1904 by Dodd, Mead & Company New York.)

MURDOCK, G. P.
  1938. Our Primitive Contemporaries. New York: Macmillan.

ORCHARD, W. C.
  1916. The Technique of Porcupine-Quill Decoration among the North American Indians. New York: Museum of the American Indian, Heye Foundation, Vol. IV, No. 1.
  1929. A. Beads and Beadwork of the American Indians. New York: Museum of the American Indian, Heye Foundation.
     B. Mohawk Burden Straps. New York: Museum of the American Indian, Heye Foundation, Indian Notes, Vol. VI.

PARKER, A. C.
  1910. A. The origin of Iroquois silversmithing. American Anthropologist, n.s., Vol. XII, No. 3.

PARKER, A. C.—*continued*

B. Iroquois Uses of Maize and Other Food Plants. Albany: Education Department Bulletin 144, New York State Museum.

1911. A. Seventh Report of the Director of the Science Division, 1910. Albany: New York State Museum, Bulletin 149.

B. Additional notes on Iroquois silversmithing. American Anthropologist, Vol. XIII, No. 2.

1912. A. Certain Iroquois tree myths and symbols. American Anthropologist, n.s., Vol. XIV, No. 4.

B. The Code of Handsome Lake, the Seneca Prophet. New York State Museum, Bulletin 163.

1922. Archaeological History of New York. Albany: New York State Museum, Bulletin Nos. 235–38, pts. 1 and 2.

1927. The amazing Iroquois. Art and Archaeology, Vol. XXIII, No. 3.

QUIMBY, G. I., JR.

1943. A subjective interpretation of some design similarities between Hopewell and northern Algonkian. American Anthropologist, Vol. 45, No. 4, pt. I.

RITCHIE, W. A.

1928. A perspective of northeastern archaeology. American Antiquity, Vol. IV, No. 2.

1943. A. Pre-Iroquoian Occupations of New York State. Rochester: Museum of Arts and Sciences.

B. Recent Advances in New York State and the Northeast. Philadelphia: Proceedings American Philosophical Society, Vol. 86, No. 2.

SCOTT, D. C.

1912. Traditional History of the Confederacy of the Six Nations. Ottawa: Proceedings and Transactions of the Royal Society of Canada, Series 3, Vol. 5.

SPECK, F. G.

1911. Huron moose hair embroidery. American Anthropologist, n.s., Vol. XIII, No. 1.

1914. The Double Curve Motive in Northeastern Algonkian Art. Ottawa: Geological Survey of Canada, Anthropological Series, Memoir 42, No. 1.

1925. Northern Elements in Iroquois and New England Art. New York: Museum of the American Indian, Heye Foundation, Indian Notes, Vol. II, No. 1.

STIRLING, M. W.

1933. Fiftieth Annual Report, Bureau of American Ethnology, 1932–33. Washington: Smithsonian Institution.

STITES, S. H.

1905. Economics of the Iroquois. Bryn Mawr, Pa.: Bryn Mawr College Monographs, Vol. 1, No. 3.

Traquair, Ramsay
  1938. Montreal and the Indian trade silver. Canadian Historical Review, Vol. XIX, No. 1.

Waugh, F. W.
  1916. Iroquois Foods and Food Preparation. Ottawa: Geological Survey of Canada, Anthropological Series, Memoir 86.

Weer, P. W.
  1937. Preliminary Notes on the Iroquoian Family. Indianapolis: Indiana Historical Society, Vol. 1.

Wintemberg, W. J.
  1931. Distinguishing Characteristics of Algonkian and Iroquoian Cultures. Ottawa: National Museum of Canada, Annual Report for 1929, Bulletin No. 67.

Wissler, Clark
  1940. Indians of the United States: Four Centuries of Their History and Culture. New York: Doubleday, Doran.

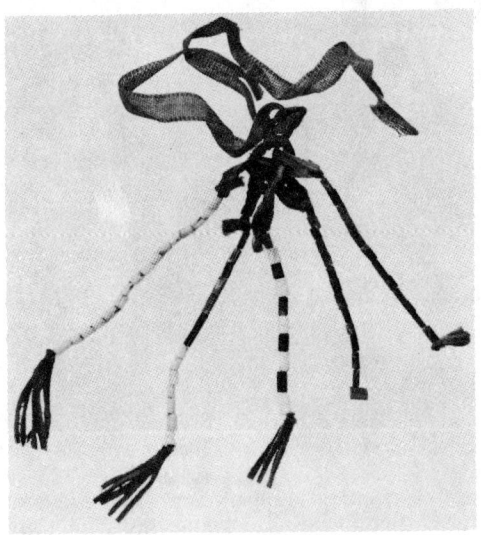

CHIEF MATRON'S WAMPUM CREDENTIALS

In the Cayuga tongue these are known as *gatkówa*. They serve in the Condolence Ceremony. Each line is symbolic; the string of alternate blue and white beads symbolizes the Chief Matron; the white string, the nominee; the half blue and half white string, the assistant or second chief; the first blue string, the female cooks for the ritual; the second blue string, the male cooks. The red ribbons are only decorative.

The last time this wampum was used to propose a nominee to fill a vacancy of a Cayuga chieftainship was when Diyohyogo, "Heron" (enrolled name, Norman General), was nominated. The strings were obtained from Kaínes, "Dropping Bundles," (Mrs. Jerry Aaron), Matron of the Deer Clan.

4172. Six Nations, 1944, F. G. Speck.

IROQUOIS HEADDRESS

This is a ceremonial headdress of five pairs of hawk feathers and an eagle feather mounted on a leather-covered wooden frame. The leather appears to be commercial "chamois," re-used, for *typewritten* on it are many Indian names.

Apparently there are not data available to indicate the use of this headdress.

3203. Maniwaki, Quebec, F. G. Speck.

The cover map is reproduced from a section of Belin's
"Partie Occidentale de la Nouvelle France ou du Canada."
1755